Kosher Gourmet Cookbook

Mildred B. Miller

and

Bascha G. Snyder

Dover Publications, Inc.

New York

To our husbands and children, with love.

Published in Canada by General Publishing Company, Ltd., 30 Lesmill Road, Don Mills, Toronto, Ontario.
Published in the United Kingdom by Constable and Company, Ltd., 3 The Lanchesters, 162–164 Fulham Palace Road, London W6 9ER.

Bibliographical Note

This Dover edition is an unabridged republication of *The Kosher Gourmet Cookbook,* first published by Paul S. Eriksson, Inc., New York, in 1974.

Library of Congress Cataloging-in-Publication Data

Miller, Mildred, 1929–
Kosher gourmet cookbook / Mildred B. Miller and Bascha G. Snyder.
p. cm.
Originally published: New York : P.S. Eriksson, 1974.
Includes index.
ISBN 0-486-28155-8 (pbk.)
1. Cookery, Jewish. 2. Menus. I. Snyder, Bascha. II. Title.
TX724.M55 1994
641.5'676—dc20 94-1531
CIP

Manufactured in the United States of America
Dover Publications, Inc., 31 East 2nd Street, Mineola, N.Y. 11501

Contents

Preface iv
Introduction vi

PART I—MENUS 1
Brunches 3
Luncheons 6
Teas 10
Cocktail Parties 11
Dinners 13
Buffets 29
Late Suppers 31
Saturday Afternoon Kiddush 33

PART II–RECIPES 35
Appetizers 37
Soups 69
Main Courses 77
Starches 126
Vegetables 139
Salads and Molds 150
Eggs 164
Breads 171
Sauces and Dressings 178
Cakes 187
Small Pastries 206
Frostings and Fillings 228
Pies and Tarts 233
Desserts 248
Frozen Desserts 274
Beverages 282
For Passover 283

Index 303

Preface

We are American Jews who love to cook but don't like to spend hours in the kitchen involved in preparing food and washing dishes. We love to entertain and want everyone to feel comfortable in our homes, as they are certain to if they themselves keep Kosher homes. If they do not, they will, on the other hand, be delightfully surprised to discover that Kosher cooking does not have to be "brown and beige" but can be sophisticated and psychedelic.

In the process of collecting our recipes we have taken cognizance of the history of the Jew in the Diaspora, the variety of his experiences, and the traditions and customs observed in his home. This background has served as the source for the emergence of the American Jewish way of life. We have sought out, investigated, and experimented with a wide selection of international recipes, and have included here those which require a minimum of time and effort to prepare, but yield a maximum of satisfaction. Simplicity is our theme, creative pleasure our object, and good food our medium.

A major section of our book is devoted to menu suggestions, for general use and for the Sabbath and Holidays. We have planned these, and the recipes, with the aim of achieving a harmony of taste, texture and color. However, we firmly believe that the most important ingredient at any table is the unharried and unhurried hostess.

We would like to share some tips that, as hostesses, we have found helpful:

*Give careful thought to detail before the party, to eliminate last-minute rush and panic.

*If you have no help, choose a menu that requires the fewest last-day preparations.

*After you have issued invitations, decide on a menu and make a list of ingredients required. Then make a shopping list, and shop as far ahead as possible.

*Make and freeze ahead of time as much as possible.

*Decide on your color scheme and coordinate your accessories.

*Always plan a centerpiece—flowers, fruits, a piece of china or another interesting ornament. This sets the mood for the party—formal, less formal, or special-occasion.

*Always use candles at an evening party, and make sure they are lit.

*If guests all know each other well, plan a shorter cocktail hour with fewer hors d'oeuvres and serve the first course at table. If guests do not know each other well before the party, plan a longer cocktail hour, more hors d'oeuvres, and no first course at the table. The guests will know each other well by dinner time!

*If one of the guests is someone well-known or prominent in his field, do not invite another guest of equal prominence who will compete. Let one guest enjoy being the center of attention.

*If guests have served themselves from a sideboard, the hostess or helper should pass seconds at the table. Guests are reluctant to leave the table, even if they would like seconds.

Read the book, try the recipes, and, as it is said in Ecclesiastes (IX:7), "Eat thy bread with joy and drink thy wine with a merry heart."

Mildred Miller
Bascha Snyder

Chestnut Hill, Mass.
September, 1974

Introduction

One of the distinctive features of Judaism is the prominent role which the home plays in the observance of the customs and rituals found in our religious tradition. The home is no less vital a factor than the synagogue in the practice of our religion. It is within the family setting that a rich and variegated pattern of ceremonials finds its expression. Daily prayers, the blessing over the bread, grace after meals, the celebration of the Sabbath and Festivals and the practices associated with them—these and a host of other observances offer ample opportunities for creating a traditional spiritual climate in the home.

The inherited body of customs and rituals has proven, in the words of Professor Mordecai M. Kaplan, to possess survival value for the Jewish people. They have served as common bonds of unity and identification and have contributed very significantly to the preservation of our people as a distinct and identifiable entity. In addition, these observances provide concrete and visible manifestations of the Jewish way of life and engender a spiritual, emotional and esthetic response which deepens one's sense of personal participation in our heritage.

Basic in the traditional pattern of the Jewish home is kashruth, the observance of the dietary laws. A home which is kosher is, quite obviously, distinctively Jewish and as a rule serves to foster further involvement in traditional observances.

It is in this light that the authors of this book are to be commended for their efforts to offer those who observe the dietary laws a rich variety of recipes which will greatly enhance the enjoyment of the food they serve in their homes. Mrs. Mildred Miller and Mrs. Bascha Snyder are devoted and loyal members of our Synagogue, and I am very happy to recommend their book as a valuable guide for the preparation of tasteful kosher menus.

Rabbi Israel J. Kazis

Temple Mishkan Tefila
Chestnut Hill, Mass.

PART ONE

Menus

The most challenging aspect of any meal preparation is deciding what to make. If you also keep a kosher home, the challenge of meal planning is that much greater. As an aid to good planning, we have designated as meat, **(M)**, dairy, **(D)**, or pareve **(P)** all menus and recipes in this book. The ingredients used can be obtained in kosher form. The menus, based upon recipes in the book, are composed with the intention of creating balanced meals, nutritionally and aesthetically, and balanced also as to effort and time expended in preparation. They should be considered points of departure, however, and we hope you will use the book creatively, varying some of the menus with other recipes found in the book.

Brunches

Brunch is an enjoyable way to entertain. It can be as elegant or as informal as you want. You set the tone. The exciting new paper goods on the market today make it possible to vary the décor according to the theme of the party, or the mood you are in. It also eliminates the need for hard-to-get help. Let your imagination run wild and have a brunch.

Bloody Marys, Screwdrivers, and Orange Juice and Champagne accompanied by salted nuts, are appropriate before all brunches.

1. D

Mushroom soufflé
Caviar pie
Salmon quiche
Smörgåsbord-style platter
Basket of croissants

Glass bowl filled with blueberries and strawberries sprinkled with kirsch
Triple chocolate squares
Apricot strips
Coffee and tea

2. D

Fish crêpes
Blintzes with bowls of sour cream and cinnamon and sugar
Smörgåsbord platter
Croissants

Strawberry cake
Lace cookies
Coffee and tea

3. M

Tomato stuffed with liver
Oven-fried potatoes
Sherried beef
Poached salmon with salmon sauce
Glass bowls individually filled with cherry tomatoes,cucumbers sliced with skin on, radishes, celery, scallions, etc.
Tea rolls

Bourbon cake or fruit cake
Black coffee and tea

4. D

Lox soufflé
Bagels and assorted cheeses
Apple German pancakes
Glass bowls of vegetables

Trifle
Coffee and tea

5. D

Kippered herring, broiled
Blintzes with sour cream
Deviled eggs (for color)
Slices of tomato, scallions, and cucumber

Parker House rolls

Sour cream twists
Coffee, tea, and milk

6. D

Scrambled eggs in chafing dishes
1. **with smoked salmon, onion, and tomato**
2. **with mushrooms**
3. **Herbed**

Pan-fried potatoes

Scones, toasted, spread with cream cheese
Swedish tea ring
Coffee, tea, and milk

7. M

Spanish Omelet
Omelet chasseur
Platter of sizzling beef fry or hot pastrami
French bread, cissel or pumpernickel bread

Hot apple strudel
Black coffee, and tea

8. D

Platters of:
Smoked white fish, carp, salmon
(Consult your dealer for amounts, usually 1/4 lb. fish per person)
Cream cheese, chive cheese, butter
Assorted bagels, rolls, home-made muffins
Dairy noodle puddings (Each 9×13" baking dish serves 12.)
Bowl of hard-cooked eggs (One per serving)

Coffee cake variations
Hot chocolate, coffee, tea, and milk

Luncheons

A ladies' luncheon should be handled lightly. It should be a culinary and aesthetic delight.

1.D *A minimum of effort.*

Cheese lollypops
Cranberry juice and lime sherbet (why not spike the cranberry juice with a little vodka?)
Fish Gormanese on lettuce cups, garnished with sliced vegetables
***Spinach soufflé, bought frozen**
Rolls

Ice cream cake, bought
Three-layer cookies—Neapolitans
Coffee and tea

***Better to take short-cuts and do it than not to do it at all.**

2. D

Sherry with caviar platter
Fish mousse in champagne sauce
Marinated vegetable platter
Rolls

Genoise
Water goblets half filled with chilled champagne, three or four fresh strawberries floating in each.

3. D

Pimm's Cup cocktail (bought at liquor store)
Cheese and crackers or warm onion board (from bakery)
Fish crêpes
Tossed salad
Rolls

Strawberry or other fruit tarts
Coffee and tea

4. D

Sherry and salted Macadamia nuts
Chilled gazpacho served in bowl of crushed ice
Mushroom soufflé
Spinach quiche
Tomato slices sprinkled with basil
Rolls

Strawberry cake

5. D

Punch bowl of Bloody Mary
Pineapple nut cheese balls
Salmon quiche (one 9 inch pie serves 6)
Platter of raw vegetables

Croissants
Dry white wine

Tinted frosted cookies
Shallow bowl of thin slices of Honeydew garnished with lime and abundance of green seedless grapes
Coffee and tea

6. D

Cranberry juice cocktail with dollop of lime sherbet
Rolled stuffed fish with white sauce
Harvard beets
Tossed green salad, oil and vinegar dressing
Basket of assorted rolls
White wine

Lime mold with strawberry ice cream
Sarah's sour cream roll-ups, frosted pink and green

7. D

Cups of hot cream of tomato soup with peanuts
Scoop of fish salad on lettuce leaf
Cocktail sauce, surrounded by:
Wedges of tomato, egg quarters, green pepper rings
Pecan rolls

Cream puffs with ice cream, hot fudge and butterscotch sauces
Coffee and tea

8. M

Fresh fruit cup with fresh mint leaf
*Chicken à la king in acorn squash (1/2 squash per person)
Tomatoes, broiled
Orange mold served on lettuce cups
Tea rolls
Sherry

Lemon chiffon pie
Coffee and tea

***Substitute: Chicken in pineapple boats**

9. M

Tomato juice with lime wedge
Salted crackers
Chicken salad
Potato sticks or chips
Cranberry-orange relish on orange slice
Roll basket

Caramel cake
Coffee and tea

1. SUMMER—D

Bowl of raspberry punch with vanilla ice cream floating on top
Assorted tarts:
- **Cheese**
- **Lime**
- **Chocolate**

2. WINTER—D

Pinwheel sandwiches, using 3 loaves of bread
- **Cheese**
- **Salmon**
- **Tuna**

Hot tea, coffee
Bavarian pies, à la Joftes:
- **1 vanilla**
- **1 Almond**

Cocktail Parties

1. M

Meatballs with chili
Hot dogs, sweet and sour
Cream puffs with chicken salad
Stuffed mushrooms
Cherry tomatoes, marinated
Caviar platter

Coffee, tea

Bird's nest cookies
Raspberry squares
Apricot squares
Chocolate brownies

2. D

Guacamole
  tacos
  chili relish
Cheese lollypops

Molded chopped herring
Mushroom roll-ups
Individual quiches Lorraine

Coffee, tea

Chocolate roll with fudge sauce
French orange coffee cake

3. D *Serves 10 people who have gathered together before going out for dinner.*

Cheese fondue with hunks of Italian bread
Herring salad à l'étoile
Sushi

Without help, serve on party paper plates, so that the hostess is ready to leave with her guests.

Dinners

Good friends and good food encourage sparkling conversation. There's no better way to spend an evening than at a dinner party at home. And you, the hostess, can have as much fun and can be as relaxed as your guests if you plan wisely. The appropriate wine should be served with each menu. Consult your wine dealer. Any menu can be adapted for family meals by adjusting the amounts and courses, and most can be served with whatever degree of formality the occasion demands.

For a formal dinner party, because your guests are dressed formally, you must provide a table setting and chair for each one. You can't balance a dinner plate on a gowned knee. We have found it simplest and relatively inexpensive to rent round tables, chairs, and tablecloths.

1. M

Pitcher of whiskey sour or gin and tonic, depending on the season

Pickled knockwurst
Guacamole and chili-tomato sauce Tacos or corn chips

Chicken breasts in rosé wine
Orange minted peas

Risotto d'Angelo

Tossed salad with artichoke hearts

Salt sticks

Paris chou. Served with a chilled sweet white wine
Demitasse or tea

2. M

Cocktails
Caviar platter

At places:Tomato stuffed with liver

Roast beef with Béarnaise sauce
Wild rice ring
Brandied fruit
Mixed green salad

Rolls
Champagne

Cherries jubilee on water ice
Petits fours (Genoise)
Demitasse or tea

3. M

Cocktails
Pretzels, nuts, etc.

Split pea soup with hot dogs, served in earthenware casserole

Beef Bourguignonne
Poppy seed noodles
Minted peas
Molded ginger ale salad or Waldorf salad

Garlic bread
Sparkling rosé

French apple pie
Demitasse or tea

4. M

Cocktails
Cherry tomatoes, marinated
Vase with crushed ice, filled with celery, carrot sticks, scallions, olives

Fish crêpes with piquant sauce

Broiled rib steaks
Burgundy mold
Asparagus

Rosé wine

Blueberry pie
Demitasse or tea

5. M

Cocktails

Gazpacho

Main course, same as #4

Crêpes Suzette or crêpes with chocolate filling

6. M

Cocktails
Chopped liver in celery stalks
Tuna paté served with crackers and party rye

Beef fondue with sauces and condiments
White rice, steamed
Carrot rings

Italian bread
Rosé wine

Lemon meringue pie
Demitasse or tea

7. M

Cocktails
Antipasto
Bread sticks

Minestrone soup
Spaghetti sauce and meatballs on rotini
Garlic bread

Sweet red wine

Beignets soufflés
Sauces

Demitasse and tea

8. M

Cocktails
Kreplach
Bowl of vegetables in ice

***Chinese beef**
Fried rice
Sherry wine
French bread
Mixed green salad with cucumber spears

Orange-raspberry baskets
or
Tangerine surprise

Platter of Scotch toffee

Tea

***Substitutes: 1. Chinese chicken**
2. Sherried beef
3. Beef in red wine

9. M

Cocktails
Hot dogs, sweet and sour
Mushrooms, stuffed
London broil, planked and ringed with
Mashed potatoes
Broiled tomatoes
Peas with mushrooms
Caesar salad

Rolls
Sparkling rosé

Assorted fruit tarts
Demitasse and tea

10. M

Cocktails
Baked salami

Sherried chicken on green noodles
Tomato-artichoke salad

Garlic bread
Dry white wine

Cherry-nut chiffon cake
Demitasse and tea

11. M

Cocktails
Caviar platter
Pretzels, nuts, etc.

Flaked haddock, rémoulade

Roast beef
Baked stuffed potato
Broccoli ring
Burgundy mold

Rolls
Champagne or rosé wine

Genoise with orange filling and apricot glaze
Demitasse and tea

12. M

Cocktails
Deviled eggs
Meat balls with horseradish

*Chicken in grapes and oranges
Barley pilaf
Mixed green salad

Rolls
Dry white wine

Pecan pie
Demitasse and tea

*Substitutes: 1. Chicken with cherries
2. Chicken chasseur

13. M

Cocktails
Cherry tomatoes, stuffed

Consommé with minced chives

*Chicken Kiev
Asparagus vinaigrette
Tomatoes, broiled
Ginger ale salad

Rolls
Dry white wine

Kahlúa pie
Demitasse and tea

*Substitute: Coq au vin

14. M *More work but worth it. Save it for that special occasion!*

Cocktails
Keep appetizers simple and salty to whet the appetite. Things that can be bought-e.g., pickled mushrooms, marinated artichokes, etc.

Giblets with meat balls in party shells

Rock Cornish hen with wild rice stuffing
Cherry-orange sauce
String beans, amandine
Tossed salad

Rolls
Champagne

Baked Alaska with water ice (made ahead and frozen)
Chocolate brownies, double-frosted

Demitasse and tea

15. M

Cocktails
Deviled eggs, #3

Tomatoes stuffed with liver

*Chicken in crumbs
Orange minted peas
Candied sweet potatoes
Cranberry-celery mold

Rolls
Sparkling rosé

Almond rolla cake
Demitasse and tea

*Substitutes: 1. Chicken in sweet and sour sauce
2. Lime-broiled chicken

16. M

Cocktails
Chopped herring on crackers
Meatballs, Chinese #2

Citrus soup, frappé

Beef-ka-bobs
Steamed white rice
Salad variation, #1

Garlic bread
Red wine

Watermelon surprise
Angel-watermelon cake
Demitasse and tea

17. M

Cocktails
Cherry tomatoes, marinated
Guacamole with tacos and chili relish

Split pea soup with sliced hot dogs

*Crown lamb roast
Oven-fried potatoes
Beets, Hawaiian
Tossed salad with mint flakes

French bread
Dry red wine

Assorted chiffon tarts
Demitasse or tea

*Substitutes: 1. Breaded veal steaks
2. Marinated veal chops

18. M

Cocktails
Mushrooms, fried
Baked salami

Lamb ka-bobs
Syrian bread filled with green salad
Rice Strauss
Zucchini

Red wine

Hot apple strudel
Demitasse and tea

19. M

Cocktails
Meat balls in chafing dish
Sardine spread on crackers

Glazed corned brisket
Casserole of hot dogs and beans
Green bean salad
Orange mold

Rolls and pumpernickel bread

Chocolate pie
Demitasse and tea

20. D

Cocktails
Cream cheese roll-ups
Herring à l'étoile

Sour cherry soup

Swordfish ka-bobs
Steamed white rice
Cole slaw

Pecan rolls
Dry white wine

Lime-pineapple pie
Coffee and tea

21. D

Cocktails
Pineapple-cheese lollypops
Mushroom roll-ups

Rolled stuffed fish
Noodle pudding, #7
Sherried spinach
Salad variation, #2

Croissants
Dry white wine

Strawberries Romanoff
Bird's nest cookies
Coffee and tea

22. D *Appropriate for Fourth of July Party.*

Cocktails
Pizza roll-ups

Fish chowder

Cold salmon with salmon sauce
Baked stuffed potatoes
Red, white and blue mold
Spiced peas

Rolls
Dry white wine

Cheese torte
Coffee and tea

23. D

Cocktails
Smoked salmon roll-ups
Cheese rounds

Fish chasseur
Noodle pudding, #6
Cauliflower in mushroom sauce
Apricot mold

Rolls
White wine

Chocolate upside-down cake
Coffee and tea

24. M

Cocktails
Salty nuts, etc.

Gazpacho

Duck à l'orange
Sweet potatoes in orange baskets
String beans with anchovies
Mixed green salad

Apricot-nut bread
Dry white wine

Lemon ice with frosted grapes
Molasses cookies
Demitasse and tea

25. D

Cocktails
Mushroom roll-ups
Onion dip

Lasagna Lenora
Antipasto

Garlic bread
White wine

Marinated pineapple
Pecan pie with ice cream
Coffee and tea

26. M

Cocktails
Fried won ton
Filled cherry tomatoes

Chinese fried chicken
Fresh bean sprouts, pea pods, bean threads, each cooked separately in small amount of salted boiling water

French bread

Paris chou
Demitasse and tea

27. M

Cocktails
Greek hors d'oeuvres

Curried chicken or chicken with kumquats
Barley pilaf
Tossed green salad
Rolls

Glazed oranges
French chocolate cake (velvet cake)
Demitasse and tea

28. M

Cocktails
Guacamole with Fritos
Warmed onion board (available in bakery)

Savory beef with vegetables
Green salad with artichoke hearts, served in cavity of
Syrian bread
Rice pilaf

Dobosch torte
Demitasse and tea

29. M

Cocktails
Assorted nuts
Dilly beans and carrots

Minestrone Soup

Beef with marinated mushrooms
Green noodles
Tossed salad
Italian bread

Tortoni
Espresso

30. M

Cocktails
Baked salami

Veal casserole
Rice
Salad platter
French bread

Individual fruit pies
Demitasse and tea

31. M

Cocktails
Greek hors d'oeuvres
Cauliflower in cocktail sauce

Veal sautéed with white wine
Marinated string bean salad
Rice
Syrian bread

Baklava
Turkish coffee and tea

32. M

Cocktails
Stuffed cucumber

Pea soup with hot dogs

Cape Cod brisket
Viennese potatoes
Egg, spinach, and beet salad
Vienna rolls

Viennese fruit torte or apple crisp
Demitasse and tea

33. D

Cocktails
Cheese fondue

Fried fish, English style
Lime mold
Noodle pudding
Platter of thin-sliced tomatoes and cucumbers
Rolls and butter

Profiteroles or trifle or Italian loaf cake
Coffee and tea

34. M INFORMAL SUPPER PARTY

Melon variations
Tuna-cheese spread (hot)

Thin steaks broiled and/or hamburg patties
Submarine-sandwich rolls
Platter of sliced onions, cucumbers, tomatoes, pickles

Beer

Chocolate delight bars
Apple cake or pound cake
Coffee and tea

35. M

Melon variations

Chili meat pies
Ratatouille

Apple crisp
Coffee and tea

36. M

Pea soup with hot dogs

Shepherd's pie
Broiled tomatoes
Broccoli ring

Surprise pudding
Coffee and tea

37. M

Pickled knockwurst

Spanish beef
Poppy seed noodles
Tossed green salad

Kahlúa pie
Coffee and tea

38. M

Fried won ton

Hawaiian chicken
Chinese noodles
Steamed white rice

Glazed oranges
Raisin-ginger snaps
Coffee and tea

Buffets

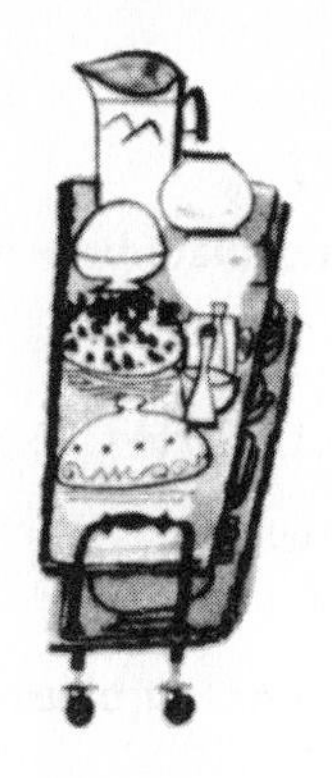

1. M *Serves 50*

Cocktails
Punch bowl of whiskey sour
Chafing dish of meatballs #1
Caviar platter
Chopped liver
Mushrooms, stuffed
Vase of chopped ice and fresh vegetables (celery, carrots, etc.)

Chicken crêpes
Cabbage, rolled
Sliced roast turkey with stuffing
Beef pastries Basket of rolls
Barley pilaf
Molded ginger-ale salad
Strawberry-rhubarb mold

Brandy snifter filled with balls of water ice
Strawberry and apricot sauces
Apricot strips, thumbprint cookies, miniature jelly rolls

Demitasse and tea

2. M *Serves 30 young adults in the summertime*

Beer keg with spigot
Pretzels, potato chips, etc.

Barbecued hamburgers, hot dogs, and beef ka-bobs
Hamburger rolls and hot dog rolls
Cole slaw
Potato salad
Relishes

Baked Alaska with water ice
Blonde brownies and chocolate brownies

3. D *Serves 16 to 20*

Punch bowl of orange delight

Antipasto, hearty
Blintzes with sour cream or hot blueberry sauce
Cinnamon twists
Cold salmon with frozen horseradish squares
Lime mold
Strawberry-cheese mold

French orange cake
Coffee-marshmallow dessert
Coffee and tea

Late Suppers

1. D

Salmon toast cups (Tuna and cheese variations)
Relishes
Noodle pudding, #5

Sour cream coffee cake
Coffee

2. D

Blueberry and apple blintzes

Ice cream soufflé

Swedish tea ring
Coffee

3. D

Mock pizzas
Potato chips
Sweet pickles

Chocolate roll with sauce
Coffee

4. M

Casserole of fried rice and beef
Orange-honey bread

Applesauce cake or chocolate cake (Devil's food)
Coffee

5. P

Eggs Foo Yong
Salad
Muffins with jelly

Coffee

6. D

Scrambled eggs
Date-nut bread

Chocolate-almond tart
Coffee

Saturday Afternoon Kiddush

1. M

Wine
Gefulte fish with horseradish

Carbonnade of brisket, cold, sliced
Cumberland sauce
Salad

Chale

Fruit torte
Tea

2. M

Wine
Chopped liver with crackers

Sauerbraten
Potato pancakes (frozen and reheated)
Green bean salad

Chale

Sacher torte
Mandel bread
Tea

3. M

Wine
Chicken soup with matzo balls

Platter of cold cuts
Cole slaw
Noodle pudding, #2

Chale

Strudel or apple squares
Tea

4. M

Wine
Gefulte fish with horseradish

Cabbage, rolled
Noodle pudding, #1
Salad variation #2

Chale

Chiffon cake
Tea

PART TWO

Appetizers

BAKED SALAMI—M

Serves six.

Skin: **1 midget salami (2-lb.)**

Make a spiral cut 1/4 inch deep around the entire salami. Place in deep pan and bake in 200° oven for 3 hours. Serve on wooden board with pumpernickel rounds and mustard.

BLINTZES

2 1/2 dozen.

Crêpes—P

Beat with wire whisk: **3 eggs**
1 t. salt
1/2 cup water

Add: **1 1/2 cups flour (all-purpose)**
1 cup water

Beat until all the ingredients are thoroughly blended. Heat a 4–inch skillet and brush with margarine. Pour in 1 tablespoon of the batter and tilt the pan immediately so that the batter will spread over the entire bottom of the pan. Bake one side until top is dry and starts to blister. Turn out onto dishtowel. Brush skillet each time before adding new batter. Repeat this process until all the crêpes are cooked.

Filling—D

Mix together: **1 lb. farmer cheese**
1/2 lb. cream cheese
1/4 lb. cottage cheese

Add: **1 egg**
pinch of salt
1 T. sugar
dash of pepper

Fill cooked side with 1 tablespoon of filling. Roll and fold in sides. Fry in butter until both sides are brown. May be frozen and heated in 400° oven for 1/2 hour. Serve with sour cream, blueberries, or cinnamon and sugar.

CABBAGE, ROLLED—M

Serves twelve. You may freeze this in serving amounts desired.

Cut off bottom core and boil in salted water to cover for 10 minutes until leaves separate easily: **1 medium head cabbage**

Drain well and separate individual leaves.
While cabbage is cooking, mix filling.

Filling

Mix together: **2 lb. ground chuck**
1 grated onion
1 egg
minced garlic
salt

freshly ground black pepper
1/4 cup water

Place small amount of meat in center of leaf (depending on size of leaf) and roll and fold in sides.

Place in bottom of deep pot: **1 sliced onion**

Place cabbage rolls with sealed edge down in pot.

Add: **1 can tomatoes**
1 can tomato sauce
1/2 cup ketchup
brown sugar
lemon juice
1 t. ginger
salt
pepper
raisins

The amount of sugar and lemon varies according to individual taste. Taste frequently and adjust the amounts. Simmer covered for 2 hours. May be frozen and reheated in the oven in shallow pan at 350° until done. This takes a long time to defrost, therefore remove from freezer the night before using.

CAVIAR MOLD—P

Serves eight to ten.

Chop and combine: **6 hard-cooked eggs**
1 medium, grated onion

Add: **1/2 cup mayonnaise**
1 t. Worcestershire sauce

Dissolve and stir until thick: **1 envelope gelatin**

In: **2 T. water**
1 T. lemon juice

Place gelatin mixture over low heat and stir until dissolved.
Pour liquid gelatin over egg mixture.

Stir in and mix well: **4 oz. black caviar**

Place in oiled 2-cup mold. When ready to serve, unmold, garnish with parsley and serve with melba toast rounds.

CAVIAR PIE—P or D

Serves ten.

In a bowl,

Mash:	**6 hard-cooked egg yolks**
Blend in:	**1 T. mayonnaise**
Press mixture into:	**lightly greased 9-inch flan pan or shallow dish**
Spread evenly:	**4-oz. jar of black caviar over egg yolk mixture**
Arrange in concentric circles, starting at outer edge:	**grated onion** **chopped chives** **chopped egg white**
Garnish center with:	**dollop of sour cream (D)** **or** **dollop of mayonnaise (P)**

Chill in refrigerator for several hours. Place flan dish on larger platter and decorate with thin slices of lemon. Cut into thin wedges and serve with melba toast or pumpernickel rounds. This looks very pretty on the coffee table and is also delicious.

CAVIAR PLATTER—P

Six to eight servings.

Arrange on sectioned tray:	**1 jar black caviar** **chopped onion**

grated yolk of hard-cooked egg
grated white of hard-cooked egg

Serve with: **toast rounds**

CHEESE FONDUE—D

Serves twelve.

In double boiler, heat: **1/2 bottle dry white wine**
1 lb. grated Swiss cheese
3 T. flour

Stir.

Flavor with: **salt**
pepper
nutmeg

Serve in chafing dish with hunks of Italian bread.

CHEESE ROUNDS—D

2 dozen.

Mix together: **1 cup mayonnaise**
3 T. grated American cheese
1 t. minced onion

Spread on: **slices of party rye**

Broil until brown and bubbly. May be frozen.

CHERRY TOMATOES, MARINATED—P

Six servings.

Mix together: **1/4 cup olive oil**
1 T. red wine vinegar

	1 clove minced garlic
	salt
	freshly ground pepper
	1/2 T. chopped parsley
Pour over:	**1 pint cherry tomatoes**

Chill.

CHERRY TOMATOES, STUFFED—P
Forty-eight.

With sharp paring knife,	
Cut off thin slice from base of	**48 cherry tomatoes**
Cut small slice from top	
Scoop out pulp.	

Place hollowed-out tomatoes in mixing bowl.

Add:	**2 T. wine vinegar**
	6 T. olive oil
	salt
	freshly ground pepper

Refrigerate one hour.

Combine:	**1 7-oz. can tuna**
	4 T. chopped capers
	2 hard-cooked eggs, finely chopped
	2 T. chopped chives
	2 t. chopped onion
	2 anchovies, chopped
	2 t. chopped parsley
	1–2 drops Tabasco sauce
	4 drops Worcestershire sauce
	2 T. mayonnaise
	1 t. lemon juice

Mash and whip to blend well.
Drain tomatoes and fill with tuna mixture.

CHICKEN CRÊPES—M

2 1/2 dozen.

For crêpe refer to recipe for Blintzes.

Filling

Sauté in pareve margarine:	**1/8 lb. fresh mushrooms, chopped**
Add:	**3 minced shallots**

Sauté until golden.

Add:	**1 cup chopped cooked chicken**
	2 T. sherry
	1 cup chicken broth

Spoon hot chicken mixture on crêpe and roll up. Place seam side down in ungreased shallow baking pan. Brush tops with melted margarine. Spoon remaining chicken around crêpes. Heat in 350° oven until hot, about 10 min. Serve two on a plate, garnished with parsley. May be frozen.

CHILI MEAT PIES—M

Sixteen to twenty.

Crust

In a large bowl,

Place:	**2 cups all-purpose flour**
	1 t. baking powder
	1/2 t. salt
Cut in with pastry blender or fork:	**2/3 cup shortening**
Sprinkle with:	**6 T. cold water, 1 t. at a time**

Mix lightly until all the flour is moistened. Gather dough together and press into a ball. Roll dough as thin as pie pastry on a floured board and cut into circles about 3 inches in diameter.

Filling

In a skillet,

Heat: **2 t. olive oil**
Add: **1 cup finely chopped onion**
1 clove finely minced garlic
1/4 cup finely chopped green pepper

Cook until the onion is slightly yellow.

Add, breaking up the lumps: **1 lb. ground beef**

Cook until meat loses its red color.

Sprinkle with: **2 t. flour**
2 t. chili powder
Add: **salt**
freshly ground pepper
3 t. tomato paste
1/8 t. red pepper
1/4 t. ground cloves
1/4 t. cumin
1/2 t. orégano

Stir well and cool thoroughly before filling pastry.
Spoon about 1 teaspoon filling in center of each pastry circle. Brush edges of circle with cold water to help seal the dough. Fold dough over and crimp the edges with a fork. With sharp knife make 2 small slits in top of each turnover to let steam escape. Repeat with remaining dough.

In skillet,

Heat at 350-375°: **enough oil to reach depth of 1 inch in pan**

Drop in turnovers, a few at a time and brown thoroughly on all sides. Drain thoroughly on paper towels. May be frozen. When ready to serve, bake in a 400° oven for about 20 minutes, until well heated. This is a versatile recipe. If you cut the rounds to 6 inches to make a more generous portion, you can serve them for lunch or supper as a main dish.

CREAM CHEESE ROLL-UPS—D

3 1/2 dozen.

Soften: **1/2 lb. cream cheese**
Moisten with: **1/4 cup milk**
Season with: **3 T. sugar**
1 t. cinnamon
Remove crust from: **1 family-size loaf white bread**

Roll slices thin with rolling pin. Spread with mixture. Roll up. May be frozen. When ready to serve, defrost. Cut each roll in half. Brush them with melted butter and heat in 400° oven until brown, about 20 minutes.

CREAM PUFFS—P

Eighteen.

Heat to boiling point in sauce pan: **1 cup water**
Stir in: **1/2 cup vegetable shortening**
1/4 t. salt
1 cup all-purpose flour

Stir constantly over low heat until mixture leaves the sides of the pan and forms a ball (about 1 minute). Remove from heat. Cool slightly.

Beat in one at a time: **4 eggs**

Beat until smooth and glassy. Drop from teaspoon on ungreased cookie sheet, 2 inches apart. Bake at 400° for 30 minutes. Allow to cool slowly. When ready to use, cut off tops and fill with desired salad fillings.

DEVILED EGGS—P

Serves six.

Halve lengthwise: **6 hard-cooked eggs**

Remove yolks and mash with desired combinations of seasonings. Refill egg whites.

Fillings

#1 Combine: **6 egg yolks**
2 T. mayonnaise
1 t. vinegar
1/2 t. salt
dash pepper
1/4 t. paprika
1/2 t. dry mustard

#2 Combine: **6 egg yolks**
2 T. mayonnaise
1 T. horseradish
1/4 t. dry mustard
1/8 t. paprika
1 t. chopped sweet pickle
1 t. parsley
1 t. salt

#3 Combine: **6 egg yolks**
1 3 1/2-oz. can tuna
1/4 cup mayonnaise
1/4 t. salt
1/8 t. pepper
2 T. cognac
1/8 t. thyme
1/4 cup chopped pecans
1 T. chopped parsley

Garnish with: **pimento**
capers

EGGS RANCHO—P

Serves two.

Line individual casseroles with: **large Fritos**

In small bowl mix: **1 4-oz. can taco sauce**
3 drops garlic juice or powder
1/8 t. orégano
1 T. olive oil

Cover Fritos with one-half of sauce.

Make a well in each and add to each: **2 eggs**

Cover with rest of sauce.
Bake uncovered in 350° oven to desired firmness, or about 15 minutes.

FILLED CUCUMBER—P

Serves six to eight.

Peel: **2 cucumbers**

Cut 1/2 inch off tip of each cucumber. Scoop out seeds and center pulp with iced-tea spoon. Pour 1/4 teaspoon salt into each cucumber and let stand for about 15 minutes to draw out moisture.

Suggested fillings:
- Deviled Eggs Filling #3
- Sardine Spread
- Tuna Pâté
- Chopped liver (M)

Stuff the cucumbers by standing them upright and spooning the filling in and packing it down. When they are both tightly packed, wrap them separately in tin foil and refrigerate for 2 hours. To serve, slice the cucumbers crosswise on a slant in slices about 1/2 inch thick. Easy to make, serve, and eat.

FISH CRÊPES—P

2 1/2 dozen.

For crêpe refer to recipe for Blintzes.

FILLING

Cook for 10 min. **1 lb. haddock filet**
2 cups water
1 carrot
1 onion
salt and pepper

Remove fish from water. Reserve water.

Combine in sauce pan: **cooked fish**
1 T. finely chopped shallots
1/2 cup dry white wine

Bring to boil and cook until wine is reduced by half.

In another sauce pan, melt:	**1/4 cup margarine**
Stir in:	**1/2 cup flour**
Add to fish mixture	**2 cups fish stock**
Add:	**1 t. finely chopped parsley** **1/2 t. chopped tarragon** **1/2 t. chopped chives**
Remove sauce pan from heat and add:	**3 egg yolks beaten with** **1/2 cup milk substitute** **2 t. anise seed** **1 t. lemon juice** **1/4 cup sherry** **salt**

Fill crêpe, roll up, and fry in margarine until both sides are brown. May be frozen and heated in 400° oven for one-half hour. Serve with Velvet Sauce and green grapes.

FISH CRÊPE #2—D

2 1/2 dozen.

Basically this is the same recipe as above, with slight variations which make it dairy.

For crêpe refer to recipe for Dessert Crêpe.

Prepare filling exactly as above, except that you may use milk instead of milk substitute, and fold in 1/4 cup heavy cream instead of sherry.

Fill crêpe, roll up and place in baking pan. Heat at 350° for 1/2 hour before serving. May be frozen and heated in 400° oven for 1/2 hour before serving. Spoon excess filling over crêpes.

GEFULTE FISH—P

Fifteen to twenty fish balls.

Have fish man grind: **5 lbs. fish filets—equal amounts of white fish and pike, and a small amount of carp or buffle carp**

In large kettle, combine: **heads, bones, and trimmings of fish**
3 onions, sliced
1 celery stalk, sliced
2 large carrots, sliced
water to cover
salt
white pepper

Bring to boil.

Combine in blender: **1 onion**
4 eggs

Add mixture to: **ground fish**
2 T. matzo meal
salt
white pepper
1/4 cup water

Shape fish mixture into balls and drop into simmering fish broth. Simmer, covered, for 2 hours. When cool, remove fish balls to platter and garnish with sliced cooked carrots. Strain broth and chill. Serve fish with jellied fish broth and fresh ground horseradish.

FISH GORMANESE—P

Serves six to eight.

In a sauce pan,

Boil together for 20 minutes: **1 lb. haddock**
large can tomatoes (#2 1/2)
salt
white pepper
garlic powder

Drain well. Chill for several hours. Flake fish with fork.

Add: **1 cup diced celery**
2 T. mayonnaise

Blend well and adjust seasoning to taste. Serve as spread with crackers or pumpernickel rounds. May also be scooped on a lettuce leaf and served as a first course at the table. A more generous portion would make a delicious luncheon dish.

FISH REMOULADE—P

Four servings.

Cook 1 lb. of haddock filet as for Fish Crêpe. Chill, flake, and serve on lettuce cup with Remoulade sauce.

GIBLETS WITH MEAT BALLS—M

Serves six to eight.

In large pot, place: **giblets and small parts of 1 chicken**
1 T. vegetable shortening

Sauté for 10 minutes.

Add: **1 chopped onion**
2 chopped carrots
2 chopped celery stalks
salt
pepper
1 t. orégano
1 bay leaf
1/2 t. basil
1/4 cup ketchup
1 t. garlic powder

Cover with water and cook covered for 10 minutes.

Drop into boiling mixture: **1 inch meat balls made from 2 lbs. of ground meat (see recipe for cabbage rolls)**

Cook covered for 40 minutes. Adjust seasoning, remove bay leaf, and serve in pastry shell or on bed of cooked white rice.

GREEK HORS D'OEUVRES

These hors d'oeuvres are made with special tissue-paper-thin sheets of phyllo pastry. It is available in speciality stores and may be purchased frozen or fresh. If frozen, defrost in its own package in the refrigerator overnight. Defrosted dough must be kept moist while being worked on or it will dry up and crack. To keep it moist, remove from paper and wrap in two dish towels, the inner one *damp,* the outer one dry, so that the moisture is kept constant. Be careful that the inner towel is not too moist, or dough will be sticky. Remove two sheets at a time and keep the rest wrapped in towels.

In skillet, melt: **1 lb. margarine**

Place sheets on flat surface, one sheet on top of the other (always use double thickness). Brush surface with melted margarine. Cut with sharp knife into 1 inch lengthwise strips. Makes about 10 strips. Place 1 teaspoon of filling at bottom edge of each strip. Roll up edge twice. Then continue to fold strip in following manner:

Take right hand corner and fold it over to the left-hand side, then left-hand corner and fold it over to the left-hand alternating until strip is used up and forms a triangle.

If you've ever folded an American flag, you'll catch on quickly. Repeat the process until all the sheets are used up. Place triangles, end side down, on ungreased cookie sheet. At this point, the hors d'oeuvres may be frozen or baked at 400° for 20 minutes, until lightly browned. If frozen, allow 30 minutes at 400°. Serve hot.

Fillings

#1 Spinach-Feta cheese-D

In large skillet,

Brown **1 1/2 cups finely chopped onions in**
1/2 cup butter

Remove from fire.

Add: **5 beaten eggs**
1/2 cup chopped scallions
1/2 lb. Feta cheese, chopped
1/2 cup fresh dill, chopped

or
1 T. dry dill
1/2 cup finely chopped parsley
2 pkgs. defrosted chopped frozen spinach
salt
freshly ground black pepper

#2 Meat-M

In large skillet,
Heat: **6 T. margarine**
Brown: **2 onions, chopped**
Add: **1 lb. ground beef. Cook until browned breaking up the lumps**

Add: **1 cup beef broth**
3 T. flour
salt
black pepper
4 T. chopped parsley
1 T. dry dill

Cook and stir until thickened. Mix all ingredients and adjust seasoning to taste.

GUACAMOLE—P

One cup.

Mash in bowl: **1 large, ripe avocado**
Season with: **1/4 t. salt**
1/2 t. garlic salt
1/4 t. chili powder
1 t. lemon juice
2 t. minced onion

Cover with thin layer of mayonnaise to keep from darkening. Chill. Just before serving, stir well. Serve with Tacos. Mexican style is to dip it first in the guacomole, then in a canned chili, tomato, and pepper sauce.

HERRING A L'ÉTOILE—D

Eight to ten servings.

Drain and rinse with cold water:	**1 13-oz. jar of herring filets**
Mix in bowl:	**herring**
	1/4 lb. smoked salmon
	1/4 cup white vinegar
	1 T. sugar
	1/2 pint sour cream
	1 sliced onion
	1/2 green pepper, diced

Store in covered jar in refrigerator 2 or 3 days. Serve with crackers or party rye.

CHOPPED HERRING—P

Eight to ten servings.

Put through grinder:	**1 13-oz. jar herring filets, drained**
	1 onion
	1 apple, pared
	3 hard-cooked eggs
Stir in:	**2 T. sugar**

Cover and store in refrigerator. May be made several days ahead. Serve on crackers or party rye.

HOT DOGS, SWEET AND SOUR—M

Heat in top of double boiler:	**3/4 cup prepared mustard**
	1 cup currant jelly
Add:	**2 pkgs. cocktail franks**

May be refrigerated or frozen. When ready to serve, heat and place in chafing dish. Serve with cocktail picks.

KNISHES—M

(1) For dough, use recipe for crêpes under Blintzes
Use meat filling under Greek Hors D'Oeuvres
Fill cooked side with 1 tablespoon of filling, roll and fold in sides.
Place on cookie sheet and brush with melted margarine or chicken fat.
Bake at 375° about 45 minutes until brown.

(2) *Dough*

In bowl,	
Place:	**2 cups flour**
Make a well and add:	**2 eggs**
	1/3 cup oil
	1 t. baking powder
	1/2 t. salt

Mix well with spoon. Form into ball. Place on floured board and knead until smooth. Roll dough thin and cut into 3 inch rounds. Place 1 teaspoon filling on each round.

KNOCKWURST, PICKLED—M

Serves twelve.

Marinade:

In sauce pan, combine:	**2 1/2 cups water**
	1 3/4 cups white vinegar
	2 T. sugar
	1 1/2 t. salt
	20 peppercorns
	16 whole allspice or 1/2 t. ground

Bring mixture to boil and reduce heat. Simmer 10 minutes. Let marinade cool to lukewarm.

Slice at an angle into 1/2 inch slices:	**1 1/2 lbs. knockwurst**
Slice thin and separate into rings:	**1 medium Bermuda onion**

In 2-quart glass jar arrange alternate layers of knockwurst slices and onion rings. Pour in the marinade. Cover jar and refrigerate for 3 days. Will keep well for several weeks in refrigerator. When serving, bring jar to coffee table. It makes an attractive conversation piece. Provide small plates and forks.

KREPLACH—M

2 dozen.

Pastry

Combine: **2 cups flour**
2 eggs
1/4 cup water
1/2 t. salt

Form into ball, place on floured board, and knead until smooth and elastic. Roll dough thin and cut into 1 inch squares. Place 1 t filling on each square. Moisten edges of dough with little water. Fold over to form triangle and press edges together to seal. Drop into boiling salted water and cook covered for 20 minutes. Drain. May be frozen. When ready to serve, heat in 350° oven.

Filling

Combine: **1/2 lb. ground meat**
1/4 cup chopped onions
salt and pepper

CHOPPED LIVER—M

Broil medium-well: **6 chicken livers**
Sauté in chicken fat: **1 large onion, chopped**
Hard cook: **3 eggs**

Put all ingredients through meat grinder. Add some of the chicken fat from onion to moisten and flavor.

Season with: **salt**
freshly ground pepper
garlic salt (optional)

Serve with crackers, rye rounds, or stuffed in celery stalks.

MEAT BALLS—M

Fifty or sixty balls.

#1 Chili

Combine: **2 lbs. ground meat**
1 egg
1 large onion, grated
salt
freshly ground pepper

Shape into 1-inch balls. Drop into simmering sauce.

Sauce:

Combine: **1 bottle chili sauce**
1/2 large jar grape jelly
juice of 1 lemon

Heat until brown. May be frozen. When ready to serve, reheat and serve in chafing dish with cocktail picks.

#2 Chinese

Combine: **2 lbs. ground meat**
1 egg
1 T. cornstarch
1 t. salt
freshly ground pepper
2 T. chopped onion

Shape into 1-inch balls and brown in small amount of oil. Drain.

Sauce:

Combine:	**1 T. oil**
	1 cup pineapple juice
Mix and add:	**3 T. cornstarch**
	1 T. soy sauce
	3 T. vinegar
	6 T. water
	1/2 cup sugar

Cook 1 minute.

Cut into pieces and add to sauce:	**4 slices canned pineapple**
	12-15 pieces green pepper

Add meatballs. May be frozen. When ready to serve, heat, and add water if sauce becomes too thick.

#3 Horseradish

Combine:	**2 lbs. ground meat**
	1/4 cup water
	1 egg
	1/2 cup bread crumbs
	2 T. prepared horseradish
	1 cup water chestnuts, chopped

Shape into 1-inch balls and brown in small amount of oil. May be frozen. When ready to serve reheat, wrapped in foil, in 350° oven for 1/2 hour. Serve with Marmalade Dip.

Dip

Combine and heat:	**1/3 cup orange marmalade**	**2 T. lemon juice**
	1 clove garlic, minced	**1/3 cup water**
	1/4 cup soy sauce	

MELON VARIATIONS—M

Serves six.

#1.

Pare, seed, and slice into 6 segments: **1 canteloupe**

Wrap a piece of corned beef around the center of the slice and sprinkle with lemon pepper.

#2.

Pare, seed, and slice into 6 segments: **1 medium honeydew**

Wrap a piece of spiced beef around center of melon slice. On a toothpick, place a maraschino cherry and slice of lime. Insert toothpick into beef.

MUSHROOMS, FRIED—P

Thirty-two pieces

Trim off tips of stems, rinse in cold water, and drain: **32 fresh white, medium-sized mushrooms**

Dredge in flour seasoned with salt and pepper.

Beat: **2 eggs**
1 t. water
1 t. peanut oil

Toss mushrooms in egg mixture until completely coated.

Coat with: **1 1/2 cups bread crumbs**

Heat oil in large skillet (375°). Deep fry mushrooms until golden brown. Drain on absorbent paper towel and serve hot with tartar sauce.

MUSHROOM ROLL-UPS—D

3 1/2 dozen.

Clean and chop fine:	**1/2 lb. fresh mushrooms**
Sauté for 5 minutes in:	**1/4 cup butter**
Blend in:	**3 T. flour**
	3/4 t. salt
	1/4 t. MSG (optional)
	1 cup light cream

Cook until thick.

Add:	**2 t. minced chives**
	1 t. lemon juice

Heat through.
Spread on bread using method described in Cream Cheese Roll-ups.

MUSHROOMS, STUFFED—P

1 dozen.

Stuffing

Break off, chop, and simmer in pareve margarine:	**stems of 1 lb. mushrooms**
Add:	**1 cup bread crumbs**
	1/2 cup corn flake crumbs
	chopped blanched almonds
	chopped scallions
Blend with:	**2 T. sherry**
	salt
	pepper to taste

Caps

Melt:	**1/4 lb. pareve margarine**
	1 t. garlic powder

Brush caps inside and out with melted mixture. Place capside down on cookie sheet. Broil 2 1/2 minutes. Stuff caps with filling. Dot with margarine and broil until brown.

ONION DIP—D

Combine: **1 pkg. pareve dried onion soup mix**
1 pint sour cream

Mix well and refrigerate. Serve with chips.

PINEAPPLE-CHEESE LOLLYPOPS—D

Twenty-four.

Cream until smooth: **1 3-oz. pkg. cream cheese**
Add and blend: **1/4 cup drained crushed pineapple**

Form into 1/2-inch balls.

Roll in: **1/4 cup finely chopped pecans**

Chill. When ready to serve, pierce each ball with pretzel stick.

PINWHEEL SANDWICHES—D

One loaf of bread makes 2 dozen.

Cheese:

Trim crust off and slice lenghthwise: **1 unsliced white bread**

Roll each side with rolling pin to flatten.

Spread with: **1/2 lb. softened cream cheese**

Place on narrow edge of each slice: **3 maraschino cherries**

Roll from narrow end.
Refrigerate or freeze. When ready to serve, slice 1/4 inch thick.

Salmon:

Proceed as above.

Spread with mixture of: **1 1-lb. can salmon**
2 T. mayonnaise
salt and pepper to taste

Place on narrow edge of each slice: **2 gherkins**

Finish as with Cheese Pinwheels, above.

Tuna:

Proceed as for Cheese Pinwheels, above.

Spread with mixture of: **2 7-oz. cans tuna**
2 T. mayonnaise
salt and pepper to taste

Place on narrow edge of each slice: **2 stuffed olives**

Finish as with Cheese Pinwheels, above.

PIZZA, MOCK—D

Twelve pieces.

Combine: **1/2 lb. American cheese**
1 t. minced onion
1 t. garlic salt
1 fresh tomato, diced
1/4 green pepper, diced
3 T. ketchup
1/4 cup mayonnaise

Place on halved English muffins. Sprinkle with orégano and broil until brown.

PIZZA ROLL-UPS—D

3 1/2 dozen.

Combine:
1/2 lb. grated American or Gruyère cheese
1 can tomato paste
1 T. olive oil
2 t. minced onion
1 garlic clove, minced
1 t. orégano
1 t. parsley flakes

Spread on bread using method described in Cream Cheese Roll-Ups. Before rolling, sprinkle with Parmesan cheese.

POTATO PANCAKES—P

Approximately 100 2-inch pancakes.

Peel and grate: **4 very large potatoes**

Drain off half liquid.

Add:
1 egg
1 T. salt
dash pepper
1 T. flour
2 t. grated onion
1/2 t. baking powder

Mix well. Drop by teaspoon into very hot oil (475°) in skillet. Brown well on both sides. May be frozen by placing pancakes between layers of aluminum foil. When ready to serve, reheat, uncovered, in 450° oven until crispy. Serve with apple sauce.

QUICHE LORRAINE—D

Serves twelve.

Line 9-inch pie plate with pastry, and bake 5 minutes.

Crumble and sprinkle over partly-baked pastry:
1 can fried onion rings
1 cup Gruyére cheese
1/4 cup Swiss cheese

Combine:
4 eggs
1 cup milk
1 cup cream
1/4 t. nutmeg
1/2 t. salt
1/4 t. white pepper

Pour over onion-cheese mixture. Bake pie 15 minutes at 425°. Reduce oven temperature to 350° for about 25 minutes until knife inserted 1 inch from pastry edge comes out clean. May be made early in the day and reheated at 350° for 10 minutes until hot.

MUSHROOM QUICHE—D

**Two 8-inch pies.*

Line 9-inch pie shell with pastry and bake 5 minutes.

In skillet, heat:
2 T. butter

Sauté:
2 cups drained mushrooms (canned)
1 T. minced onion

In bowl, beat:
4 eggs
salt, pepper to taste
1 t. Dijon mustard

Add:
1 T. flour
2 cups heavy cream
4 oz. Port Salut cheese, grated

Fold in mushroom mixture. Pour into shell. Bake at 375°, 35–40 minutes, until knife inserted 1 inch from pastry edge comes out clean.

*You may use one pie and freeze one for another time. Remove from freezer and place immediately in oven to bake at 375° for 3/4 hour, until well heated through.

SPINACH QUICHE—D

**Makes two 8-inch pies. Each serves 8 or 10.*

Line 2 8-inch pie plates with pastry for pie crust (see Index) and bake 5 minutes.

In a skillet, heat:	**2 T. butter**
Sauté:	**1 pkg. chopped frozen spinach, cooked and drained**
	1 pkg. chopped frozen chives
	salt and pepper to taste
In bowl, beat:	**4 eggs**
Add:	**1 T. flour**
	2 cups heavy cream
	5 T. Swiss cheese, grated
	salt, pepper
	1/4 t. nutmeg

Fold in spinach mixture. Pour into shell. Bake at 375°, 35–40 minutes, until knife inserted 1 inch from pastry edge comes out clean.
*You may use one pie and freeze one for another time. Remove from freezer and place immediately in oven and bake at 375° for 3/4 hour, until well heated through.

SALMON CROQUETTES—P

2 1/2 dozen.

Combine:	**1 large can red salmon**
	1 onion, grated
	juice of 1/2 lemon
	4 well-beaten eggs

1 t. salt
freshly ground pepper
1 drop Tabasco sauce
1/2–3/4 cup matzo meal

Mix well and drop by teaspoon into hot oil (375°). Fry until brown on both sides. May be frozen and reheated on cookie sheet in 400° oven 20–30 min. Serve with Remoulade Sauce.

SMOKED SALMON ROLL-UPS—D

Serves ten to twelve.

Spread: **8 oz. cream cheese**
On: **1/2 lb. large slices smoked salmon**
Place on each: **1 red onion slice**

Roll up. Refrigerate or freeze. Slice and spread on Melba toast rounds.

SARDINE SPREAD—P

Ten to twelve servings.

Blend well: **1 tin sardines**
1 T. anchovy paste
1 t. lemon juice
1 T. orange juice
1 t. Worcestershire sauce
1/4 cup cucumber
3 T. mayonnaise

Refrigerate and serve on crackers.

MOCK SEAFOOD COCKTAIL—P

Break up a head of cauliflower into flowerets. Wash and drain well. Arrange on large serving platter and place small bowl of seafood cocktail sauce in center. Serve chilled.

SUSHI—D

Thirty-six squares.

In sauce pan, combine and bring to boil: **1 1/3 cups water**
1 T. prepared horseradish
1 T. butter
3/4 t. salt
dash of pepper

Stir in: **1 1/3 cups packaged, pre-cooked rice**

Cover. Remove from heat and let stand 5 minutes. Cool slightly.

Stir in: **1 cup sour cream**
2 T. anchovies, chopped
2 T. ripe olives, chopped

Press mixture into buttered 8-inch-square pan. Cover and chill. Cut into small squares. Garnish each square with olive slice.

TOMATOES STUFFED WITH LIVER—M

Serves eight.

Broil and set aside: **1 1/2 lbs. chicken livers**
Wash and dry: **8 firm tomatoes, large**

Cut off thin slice from stem end and scoop out pulp. Season scooped tomatoes lightly with salt and pepper and set aside.

Wash and dry: **1/2 lb. fresh mushrooms**
Reserve: **8 caps**

Chop: **rest of mushrooms**
Melt: **2 T. margarine**
Add, and cook 3 minutes: **1 medium-sized onion, minced, and the chopped mushrooms**
Add: **1/2 cup bread crumbs**
1/2 tomato pulp
1 T. chopped parsley
1 t. salt
1/8 t. pepper

Cook 3 more minutes.

Cut in bite-size pieces and add to tomato mixture: **the broiled chicken livers**
2 T. white wine

Fill tomato shells with liver mixture. Dot with margarine and top with 8 sautéed mushroom caps. Place in well-greased pan. Bake at 350° 20 min.

TUNA CHEESE SPREAD—D

Eight to ten servings.

Cut into pieces and melt in top of double boiler: **1/2 lb. American cheese**
Remove from heat and add: **1 7-oz. can tuna fish**
1/2 cup mayonnaise
1/2 t. Worcestershire sauce

Serve chilled or hot on crackers.

TUNA PÂTÉ—P

Ten to twelve servings.

Place in blender: **1 7-oz. can tuna, drained**
2 small sweet pickles
3 T. diced celery

juice of 1/2 lemon
1 T. mayonnaise

Blend thoroughly and chill. Serve with crackers. May be also served with tacos and chili relish.

FRIED WON TON M

120 pieces

Use package of frozen won ton leaves. Divide each square into fourths. You will have 4 small squares from each leaf. Place leaf on work surface so that it lies in diamond shape. Place teaspoon of filling on top half of diamond. Bring bottom point to within 1/2 inch of top point. Moisten pastry edge with beaten egg (to seal) and fold side edges over—like an envelope flap.

In a large skillet, heat to 425°: **1 inch of vegetable oil**

Drop a few won ton at a time into hot oil. Turn to brown on both sides. They brown in very few minutes, so watch carefully. Lift browned won ton from oil with slotted spoon. Place on paper towel to drain. Repeat until all won ton are fried. These freeze well. When ready to serve, heat in 350° oven for ten minutes.

FILLING

In a bowl combine:

1 1/2 lbs. ground beef
small can water chestnuts, chopped
1 pkg. frozen spinach, chopped
1 bunch scallions, chopped
1 T. soy sauce
1 T. sherry wine
salt and pepper to taste

Soups

CABBAGE SOUP, SWEET AND SOUR—M

Ten servings.

Place in large soup kettle and bring to boil:	**2 qts. water** **1 lb. short ribs** **1 soup bone**

Skim off top with paper towel.

Add to boiling water:	**1 cabbage, shredded** **2 whole onions** **1 large can tomatoes** **juice of 1 or 2 lemons** **1/2 cup sugar** **1 clove garlic** **1 T. salt**

Let simmer for several hours. Adjust seasoning after 1 hour. Remove meat, bones, garlic clove, and onions.

CHICKEN SOUP WITH MATZO BALLS—M

Ten servings.

Bring to boil:	**2 qts. water**
Add:	**1 4-lb. pullet and parts**
	1 whole onion
	1 leek
	1 parsnip
	2 carrots, sliced
	3 stalks celery with leaves
	2 T. dried chopped parsley
	2 T. salt
	pepper (optional)

Cook over medium heat until chicken is done (about 1 1/2 hours). Remove chicken, parts, vegetables except sliced carrots, and adjust seasoning. Chill, remove fat from top and reheat.

MATZO BALLS

Serves ten.

#1 Beat:	**3 eggs**
	1 t. salt
Gradually add:	**3/4 cup matzo meal**

With moistened hands, shape into 1-inch balls and drop into rapidly boiling salted water to which 1 tablespoon of chicken fat has been added. Cover and cook 20 min. Remove from water and put into soup.

#2 Beat:	**3 eggs**
	1 T. water
	1 T. top of chicken soup
	1 T. salt
	pepper
Gradually add:	**1/2 cup matzo meal**

Place in refrigerator for 1/2 hour until mixture becomes thick enough to roll into balls. Form balls and drop into boiling chicken soup. Cook for 20 minutes.

CITRUS SOUP, FRAPPÉ—P

Serves six.

Soften: **1 1/2 T. unflavored gelatin**
In: **1/4 cup red wine**

Dissolve mixture over hot water.

Stir in, strained: **1 cup orange juice**
3/4 cup raspberry juice
1/4 cup lemon juice

Add: **1 cup sauterne**
2 T. kirsch
dash of salt
nutmeg to taste
1 cup orange sections

Chill and freeze for at least 2 hours. When ready to serve, break up jelly with fork and serve soup in chilled cups. Garnish with thin slices of orange dipped in sugar.

FISH CHOWDER

Serves six to eight.

#1.—**P** Place in large soup kettle: **1 lb. haddock**
2 cups water
1 small onion, chopped
1 clove garlic, minced
2 T. green pepper, chopped
2 T. Pareve margarine
2 cups canned tomatoes
2 medium potatoes, diced
1/2 cup celery, minced
1 bay leaf
1 T. salt
1/8 t. freshly ground pepper
1 T. parsley flakes

Cook until potatoes are tender.

#2.—**D** Place in large soup kettle:

1 lb. haddock
1 carrot, diced
1 medium onion, chopped
2 stalks celery, chopped
1 large potato, diced
1 T. salt
freshly ground pepper
1 bay leaf
water to cover

Cook until potatoes are tender.

Add:

3 cups milk
1 cup cream
4 T. butter
1/4 cup egg barley

May be refrigerated or frozen. When ready to serve, reheat. A small can of peas or box of frozen peas may be added.

GAZPACHO—P

Serves eight to ten, in small cups.

Put into blender:

1/2 cup diced green pepper
1/2 cup chopped onion
1 garlic clove
1/2 cup diced cucumber
1/3 cup vinegar
3 T. olive oil
1/8 t. freshly ground pepper
1 can pareve tomato soup
1 can water

Blend well. Chill. Garnish with croutons, diced cucumber, or minced green pepper. Serve with bread sticks. Keeps in the refrigerator for many days.

MINESTRONE—M

Serves twelve.

Boil for 2 minutes: **1/2 lb. dry white beans**

Remove from heat, cover and soak 1 hour before using as further directed.

In large soup kettle place: **2 qts. water**
1 lb. short ribs
1 soup bone

Bring to boil and skim off top with paper towel.

Add: **1 clove garlic, chopped**
1 onion, chopped
1 leek, diced
1 t. chopped parsley
1 t. chopped basil
1 T. tomato paste
1 large can tomatoes
3 stalks celery, chopped
2 carrots, sliced
2 potatoes, diced
1 small turnip, peeled, diced
1/4 small cabbage, shredded
2 zucchini, diced
salt to taste
1/2 t. fresh pepper

Cook slowly for 45 minutes to 1 hour.

Add: **soaked beans**
1 cup elbow macaroni

Cook 10 minutes or until tender. Adjust seasoning.

SOUR CHERRY SOUP—D

Six or eight servings.

Cook 10 to 15 minutes: **2 lbs. sour cherries, canned in water and pitted**
1 cup sugar
1 stick cinnamon

Remove cinnamon and blend in: **2 T. flour**
6 T. cold water

Put into blender: **soup mixture**
3 T. cold water

Blend until smooth.

Add: **3 cups water**

Return to pot and heat to boiling. Chill.

Before serving, add: **1 cup heavy cream**
1 cup dry red wine

Place in serving bowls and add a dollop of whipped cream.

SPLIT PEA SOUP WITH SLICED HOT DOGS—M

Eight to ten servings.

Place in large soup kettle: **2 qts. water**
1 lb. shortribs
1 soup bone

Bring to boil and skim off top with paper towel.

Add: **1 box green split peas**
1 onion, whole
2 celery stalks, whole
1 carrot, whole
1 parsnip, whole
1 bay leaf
1 T. salt
freshly ground pepper

Cook slowly until meat is tender and split peas are completely dissolved, about 2 hours.

Ten minutes before serving, add: **5 or 6 sliced hot dogs**

May be made a day ahead and reheated.

TOMATO SOUP, CREAMED WITH PEANUTS—D

Four to six servings.

Heat well: **1 can pareve tomato soup**
1 can milk

Place in serving bowls and float 6 or 8 salted peanuts on each portion. To keep the soup pareve, add 1 can water instead of milk.

Main Courses

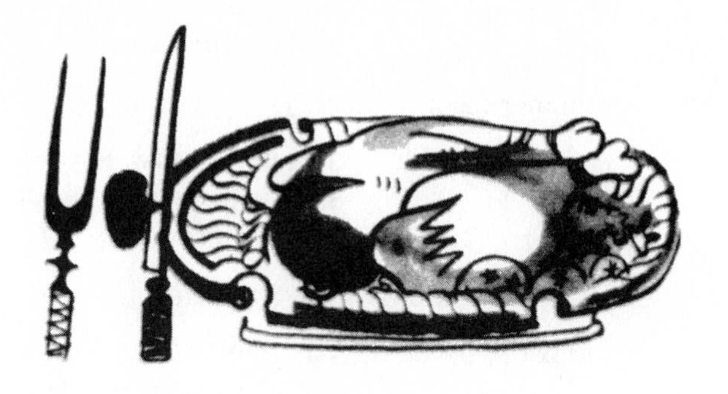

BEEF

BEEF BOURGUIGNONNE—M

Serves six.

Combine in large heavy casserole:	**2 lbs. cubed chuck**
	3 or 4 carrots, cut up
	1 cup chopped celery
	2 onions, sliced
	2 cups canned tomatoes
	1 cup tomato sauce
	1 clove garlic
	salt and pepper
	3 T. minute tapioca
	1 T. sugar
	1/2 cup red wine
Cook at 250° for 4 hours.	
During last hour, add:	**1 can mushrooms**
	2 cans small white potatoes

May be frozen. When ready to serve, reheat in oven.

CHINESE BEEF—M

Serves six.

Heat in skillet:	**4 T. salad oil**
Add and brown on all sides:	**2 lbs. thin-sliced shoulder, blade steak or chuck**
	1 clove garlic
	2 t. salt
	dash pepper
	1/2 t. ground pepper

Cover tightly and simmer for 5 minutes.

Add:	**3 fresh tomatoes, quartered**
	3 green peppers in chunks
	1 lb. bean sprouts

Bring to boil, cover, and cook briskly for 5 minutes.

Make paste of:	**1 T. cornstarch**
	1/4 cup water and 1/4 cup soy sauce

Add paste to beef mixture and cook until sauce thickens (about 5 minutes). Stir occasionally.

BEEF FONDUE—M

Six servings. (Never attempt this for more than six).

Use 2–2 1/2 pounds diced rib or shoulder steak.
You will need one fondue pot for every two guests. Each guest will need two forks, one with a long shaft.

Fill each fondue pot with:	**Salad oil kept piping hot over alcohol flame.**
Place between every two guests:	**bowl of bite-sized pieces of meat**
	variety of sauces

Each guest, using the long-handled fork, puts a piece of beef into boiling oil and cooks it until done as desired. When done, he uses the second fork and dips beef into one of offered sauces.

#1 *Garlic Sauce* 1/2 cup

Combine and beat with fork:
1/2 cup softened margarine
3 cloves garlic, minced
salt and pepper to taste

Refrigerate or freeze. Serve at room temperature.

#2 *Tomato Sauce* 1 1/2 cups

In sauce pan combine:
1 8-oz. can tomato sauce
1/3 cup steak sauce
2 T. brown sugar
2 T. salad oil

Refrigerate or freeze. When ready to serve, bring to boil. Serve hot.

#3 *Horseradish Sauce* 1 1/4 cups

Combine:
1 cup mayonnaise
3 T. white horseradish
1/4 t. salt
dash paprika

Refrigerate until serving time.

Suggested condiments:
chutney
slivered almonds
grated coconut
pineapple chunks
parsley
pickled relish
cocktail onions
olives
salted peanuts
chives

Provide a ramekin of rice for each guest.

ITALIAN BEEF—M

Serves four to six.

In heavy sauce pan, heat: **1/4 cup olive oil**
Brown quickly on all sides: **3 lbs. chuck**
Add: **1 carrot, chopped**
1 stalk celery, chopped
1 onion, chopped
2 cloves garlic, chopped
2 bay leaves
salt
freshly ground pepper

Cook uncovered over low heat for 4 minutes.

Add: **1 cup red wine**
1 small can tomato paste
2 cups warm beef broth
1 can mushrooms

Cover and bring to boil. Continue cooking on low heat, covered until meat is tender, (about 2 1/2 hours). Stir occasionally, basting meat from time to time. If gravy becomes too thick, add more warm beef broth. When meat is done, remove from pan. Serve gravy, unstrained, separately. Serve with wide noodles.

BEEF-KA-BOBS—M

Serves six.

Marinate in desired sauce: **2 lbs. cubed beef**

Sauces:

#1. 1 cup soy sauce, 4 T. molasses, 1 T. garlic juice
#2. 1/2 cup brown sugar, 1/4 cup vinegar, 1/2 cup ketchup. See marinades for London Broil.

Thread skewers with alternate pieces of: **beef**
cherry tomatoes

1 can small round onions
1 can small white potatoes
pieces of green pepper
mushroom caps

Brush skewer with marinade sauce. Place over charcoal or under broiler. Turn often until meat is done to your liking. Serve with rice.

BEEF IN MARINATED MUSHROOMS—M

Serves six.

In skillet heat:	**3 T. oil**
Add and sauté:	**2 onions, sliced**
Add:	**3 lbs. shoulder steak, thinly sliced, 2 × 3″**
	1 6-oz. can tomato paste
	1 6-oz. jar marinated mushrooms with the juice
	salt and pepper to taste

Cook 10 minutes, heat through and serve.

BEEF PASTRIES—M

Serves six.

Make recipe for 2-crust pie. Roll 1/4 inches thick and cut into 8 4-inch circles.

Beef Filling

Brown in 4 T. margarine:	**2 lbs. coarsely ground meat**
	1 onion, finely chopped
	1 lb. mushrooms, finely chopped
Add:	**1 T. salt**
	pepper
	2 t. dry mustard

2 garlic cloves, minced
1 cup ketchup
2 T. bottled steak sauce
2 t. parsley, chopped
2 t. orégano
1/2 t. rosemary
2 bay leaves, crumbled

Simmer 5 minutes. Remove from heat. Spread beef mixture on pastry rounds. Fold over in half. Moisten and seal edges. Place in greased baking dish. Brush tops with beaten egg. Dot with margarine and sprinkle with paprika. May be frozen. When ready to serve, bake in 350 ° oven until brown. About 30 min.

BEEF IN RED WINE—M

Six servings.

In large skillet, melt: **4 T. margarine**
Blend with: **4 T. flour**

Blend until smooth and brown.

Add: **1 1/2 cups beef broth**
1/2 cup red wine

Heat and stir until hot.

Add: **2 lbs. thin-sliced shoulder, blade steak or chuck**

Cook until meat is tender, about 10 or 15 min.

SAVORY BEEF WITH VEGETABLES—M

Serves six.

In skillet heat: **1 stick margarine**
3 T. seasoned salt

Add: **1 cup onion, cut in julienne strips**
2 green peppers, cut in julienne strips
2 large tomatoes, cut into wedges
12 medium fresh mushrooms, sliced

Stir and mix gently a few seconds.

Add: **3 lbs. chuck, cut into 1 inch cubes**

Sauté until beef is browned and vegetables are tender,

Add: **1/2 cup good sherry, unsalted**

For more colorful vegetables, reserve some of the green pepper and tomato and add to skillet just before putting in the sherry.

SHERRIED BEEF—M

Serves six.

Heat in skillet: **4 T. peanut oil**
Sauté slightly: **4 cups onion rings, thinly sliced**
Add: **3 T. soy sauce**
1 t. sugar
4 t. sherry

Continue to heat a few seconds. Remove from pan.

Dredge: **2 lbs. thin-sliced shoulder steak**
In: **6 t. cornstarch**
3 T. soy sauce
3 t. sherry
Heat pan and add: **6 T. peanut oil**

Sauté beef until brown. Add onions, heat through and serve.

SPANISH BEEF—M

Serves four.

This is a stunning dish to prepare in the fall, when pumpkins and squash are in season. The pumpkin shell becomes the casserole dish.

Wash well: **a 10- to 12-lb. pumpkin**

With a sharp knife, cut into the top of the pumpkin to create a lid 6 or 7 inches in diameter. Leave the stem intact as a handle. Lift out the lid and scrape the seeds and stringy fibers from the lid and the pumpkin shell.

Brush inside of pumpkin with: **1/2 cup margarine**
Sprinkle with: **1 cup sugar**

Tip pumpkin from side to side to make sugar adhere to margarine. Put the lid back in place. Place pumpkin in shallow roasting pan and bake at 375° for 45 minutes until tender but firm enough to hold filling.

In large heavy pot, heat: **2 T. oil**
Add: **2 lbs. chuck, cut into cubes**

Brown on all sides. Remove meat from pot and set aside.

To the remaining oil, add: **1 cup chopped onions**
1/2 cup chopped green pepper
1/2 t.finely chopped garlic

Cook over moderate heat stirring constantly for about 5 minutes, or until vegetables are soft but not brown.

Add: **4 cups beef stock**

Bring to boil over high heat.

Return meat to pan and stir in: **1 cup canned tomatoes, chopped and drained**
1/2 t. orégano
1 bay leaf
1 t. salt
freshly ground black pepper

Cover the pan and simmer for 15 minutes.

Add: **1 1/2 lbs. sweet potatoes, cubed**
1 1/2 white potatoes, cubed

Cover and cook 15 minutes.

Add: **1/2 lb. zucchini, unpeeled and sliced**

Cover and cook 10 minutes.

Add: **3 ears of corn, cut into 1-inch rounds**
8 canned peach halves (optional)

Cover and cook 5 minutes. Pour beef and vegetables carefully into baked pumpkin. Cover with lid and bake at 375° for 15 minutes.

TERIYAKI—M

Serves six.

Cut into thin strips: **2 lbs. steak (rib, shoulder or blade)**
Marinate for two hours in: **1 cup soy sauce**
1/2 cup sherry
1 medium onion, chopped fine
2 cloves garlic, chopped fine
2 T. sugar
2 t. ginger

Thread meat on skewers and broil quickly on both sides over charcoal or in preheated broiler. Serve hot.

ROAST BEEF—M

Plan one-half pound per person.

Dredge in garlic-seasoned flour: **1 rib roast of beef**

Place fat side up in open pan in preheated oven, 450°. Do not add water. Do not cover. Do not baste. After 15 minutes, reduce heat to 350°. Allow 15 minutes cooking time for each pound of meat. If taken directly from freezer, increase cooking time 10 to 15 minutes per pound. Serve with Béarnaise Sauce and popovers.

ROAST BEEF #2—M

Pre-heat oven to 500°. Place meat fat-side up in open pan, in preheated oven. Allow five minutes per pound at 500°. Shut off oven. *Do not open oven door.* After 1 1/2 hours remove meat from oven.
Roasting the meat this way makes it brown and crusty on the outside and pink and juicy in the center. If you prefer meat very rare, remove from oven after 1 hour and 15 minutes.

LONDON BROIL—M

Serves four.

Have butcher cut a 3-lb. shoulder roast 3 inches thick. Marinate it for several hours, in refrigerator, in one of the following:

Marinades

#1. Bottle of French salad dressing.
#2. 1 cup soy sauce, 4 T. honey, 1 T. garlic juice, salt, pepper.
#3. 1 cup soy sauce, 1/4 cup pineapple juice, 1 t. ginger.
#4. 1 jar sweet and sour sauce and 1/2 cup soy sauce.
#5. Brush with oil mixed with 1 t. salt, pepper, garlic salt.

Place on lowest rack of broiler and broil at 450° for 20 minutes. Turn meat over and broil 20 more minutes. Slice on the diagonal.

PLANKED STEAK—M

Serves four.

Boil and mash:	**2 potatoes**
Broil to doneness you prefer:	**1 thick rib steak (1 1/2")**

Place on wooden plank or sizzle platter.

Cut in half, brush with margarine, salt, basil: **2 tomatoes**
Make border of: **mashed potatoes brushed with egg white and paprika**

Bake at 450° until potato is golden brown. Arrange alternately a border of cooked mushroom caps and peas. Slice on the diagonal and serve immediately.

TOP OF RIB, STUFFED—M

Six servings.

Have butcher pound or score on both sides: **2-lb. top of rib**
In skillet, heat: **2 T. pareve margarine**
1/2 large onion, chopped
1 clove garlic, minced
1/2 cup chopped mushrooms
Cook 3 minutes and add: **1/4 cup chopped parsley**
1 1/2 cup soft bread cubes
1/2 t. orégano
1/4 t. basil
1/2 t. salt
freshly ground black pepper
1 egg, slightly beaten

Spread mixture on meat. Roll lengthwise as for jelly roll and tie with string at 2 inch intervals. Brown meat on both sides in a little oil in skillet or heavy Dutch oven.

Add: **1/2 cup red wine**

Cover and bake 2 hours. To serve, cut into 1 inch slices and serve with pan drippings.

CAPE COD BRISKET—M

Serves eight.

In roasting pan, place:	**large piece of heavy-duty tin foil, allowing enough to wrap meat tightly**
Place on tin foil:	**6-lb. single brisket**
Sprinkle over meat:	**1 pkg. onion soup mix**
Spoon over meat:	**1 lb. can whole cranberries**

Fold over sides of foil and tightly seal ends together. Do not open during roasting. Roast at 375° for 3 hours. Unwrap and serve. Place sliced meat on pre-heated platter and spoon some sauce over the meat. Serve the rest of the sauce in a gravy boat.

CARBONNADE OF BRISKET—M

Ten servings.

Marinate overnight in 1 1/2 cups beer, 1/2 t. ground ginger:	**1 1/2 cups dried prunes** **1 1/2 cups dried apricots**
In large heavy covered pot, brown on all sides:	**6-lb. single brisket**
Add and brown:	**2 onions, sliced**
Add:	**1/4 cup water**

Simmer 1 hour. Cool. Remove from stock and slice. Return meat to stock

Add:	**1/2 t. cinnamon** **dash pepper** **1/3 cup honey** **1/2 cup brown sugar**

Simmer 1 hour, covered.

Add:	**10 medium potatoes, sliced** **the prunes and apricots** **marinade**

Simmer covered about 30 minutes.
To serve, place meat slices down middle of platter and arrange potatoes and fruit around meat.

GLAZED CORNED BRISKET—M

Eight servings.

Place in large pot and cover with cold water: **6-lb. corned brisket**

Bring to boil. Taste water. If too salty, spill out water and refill pot with water to cover. Cook until almost done—two hours. Remove from pot and place in baking pan. Score (cut fat surface into squares or diamonds). Stud each square with whole clove.

Spread with paste of: **1 cup brown sugar**
1 t. dry mustard
3 T. vinegar, honey, or fruit syrup

Baste occasionally with fruit juice or cider. Bake 45 minutes at 350°.

SAUERBRATEN—M

Serves eight to ten.

In large bowl marinate: **4 lbs. boneless chuck**

In: **1 pint red wine vinegar**
2 1/2 pints water
2 onions, sliced
1 carrot, sliced
1 stalk celery, chopped
4 cloves
4 peppercorns
1 T. salt
1/2 t. pepper
2 bay leaves

Cover and refrigerate for *4 days.* On 5th day, drain meat and reserve marinade.

Sauté meat in heavy pan in: **8 T. margarine**
Add: **marinade**

Cover tightly and simmer until meat is tender, 2 1/2 or 3 hours. Remove meat and keep it hot.

Thicken gravy with: **5 T. flour**
1 T. sugar
8–10 ginger snaps, crushed

Serve sliced and pour gravy over meat. Serve with potato pancakes.

SWEET AND SOUR BRISKET—M

Serves ten.

Place in heavy skillet and brown on all sides: **6-lb. single brisket**
Add and brown: **2 onions, sliced**
1 clove garlic, minced
3/4 cup brown sugar
1/2 cup vinegar
1 cup ketchup
1 cup water
1 T. salt
freseshly ground pepper

Cook covered until meat is tender, about 2 1/2 or 3 hours.

SHEPHERD'S PIE—M

Serves six.

Place in bowl: **3 lbs. ground beef**
Add: **1 egg**
1 onion grated (you can mix egg

and onion in an electric blender for a smoother texture)

Add and mix with beef: **1/4 cup water**
salt and pepper to taste
1 t. garlic powder (optional)
1 T. Worcestershire sauce

In 1 1/2-quart pyrex baking dish, place 1/3 of ground beef mixture. Along center place two whole, hard-cooked, shelled eggs. Place remaining 2/3 of meat over eggs and shape into loaf. Place one bay leaf on top of meat loaf. Bake at 350° for 1 hour.

Mashed Potato crust

In bowl place: **3 cooked potatoes, peeled and well mashed.**

Add: **salt and pepper to taste**
1 raw egg
1/8 lb. margarine

Beat in mixer until fluffy.
Ten minutes before meat loaf is done, spread potato mixture over loaf and sprinkle with paprika. Continue baking until potatoes become lightly browned and crusty.
Serve on platter and slice crosswise. Each slice will have a topping of potato, a thick rim of meat, and a slice of egg in the center. Very attractive, very tasty, and very easy.

SPAGHETTI AND MEAT BALLS—M

Serves eight.

In heavy skillet, heat: **1 T. olive oil**
1/2 cup ground beef

Add and sauté: **2 onions, chopped**
1/2 green pepper, chopped
clove garlic, chopped
1 t. salt
freshly ground pepper
1 t. orégano

Add: **1 large can Italian tomatoes**
1 8-oz. can tomato sauce
1 can tomato paste
1 T. sugar

Simmer covered for several hours. Adjust seasoning. Add orégano again just before serving. Add meatballs and serve over one pound cooked spaghetti or rotini.

Meatballs—M

Mix together: **2 lbs. ground meat**
1 egg
1 t. salt
freshly ground pepper
finely chopped parsley
1/4 cup water

Form into balls and pan fry in hot oil. Drain liquid before adding balls to sauce.

BARBECUED SHORT RIBS—M

Six servings.

Place in deep bowl: **6 lbs. short ribs, cut into serving pieces**

Mix and pour over ribs: **4 T. prepared mustard**
1 T. salt
1 t. chili powder
1 t. sugar
4 T. lemon juice
1/2 cup oil
1 clove garlic, crushed
freshly ground black pepper
2 small onions, chopped

Cover and refrigerate several hours, turning meat once or twice. Drain, reserving the marinade. Preheat oven to 450°. Arrange ribs on rack in roasting pan and bake 30 minutes. Reduce oven temperature to 350° and add reserved marinade to ribs. Cover and bake until tender, about 1 1/2 hours. Uncover and bake until fat on ribs is crisp. Pour off fat from pan.

Put in sauce pan: **1–1/3 cups canned beef broth**

Boil two minutes.
Thicken broth with flour mixed with a little water and serve with ribs.

CASSEROLE OF FRIED RICE AND BEEF—M

Serves six to eight.

Heat in skillet: **2 T. peanut oil**
With a fork, swish in: **2 raw eggs**
Add and sauté for a short time: **3 cups cooked, left-over roast beef, cubed**
4 stalks celery, sliced on the diagonal
1 cup onion, chopped
1/2 cup green pepper, sliced
Add: **3 cups beef broth**
4 T. soy sauce
2 T. bead molasses
salt
1 t. garlic juice
3 cups packaged pre-cooked rice

Cover and heat on low flame. Serve immediately.

CASSEROLE OF HOT DOGS AND BEANS—M

Serves six to eight.

Place in casserole: **3 jars pareve baked beans**
2 pkgs. cocktail franks
1/4 cup prepared mustard
1/4 cup ketchup

1/4 cup light molasses
1/2 cup pickle relish

Heat thoroughly in 350° oven.

SWEET AND SOUR TONGUE—M

Serves six.

Cook, cool, and slice: **3 1/2 lbs. pickled tongue**
In sauce pan, heat marinade of: **1 can cranberry jelly**
1/2 cup chili sauce
1/2 cup hot water
3/4 cup white raisins

Cook until jelly melts. Add sliced tongue to marinade. May be frozen. When ready to serve, reheat at 350° until well heated throughout.

BREADED VEAL STEAK—M

Serves six.

Dip into beaten egg diluted with 2 tablespoons water: **6 veal steaks, pounded thin**
Roll in: **1 cup bread crumbs**
1 T. chopped parsley
1 t. orégano
salt
freshly ground pepper

Melt 1/4 cup margarine in skillet. Add steaks and cook over moderate heat until tender, 15 minutes on each side. Serve with heated pareve tomato and mushroom sauce.

VEAL CASSEROLE—M

Serves six.

In large skillet heat: **1/2 cup vegetable oil**
Cut into 1 inch strips: **3 lbs. veal steaks**
Sprinkle meat with: **salt and pepper**

Add meat to skillet and brown well. Transfer meat to 3-quart casserole.

Add to skillet and heat: **1/2 cup vegetable oil**
Add: **3/4 cup flour**

Cook, stirring until flour is blended.

Add and cook until soft: **3 cups chopped onion**
1 cup tomato paste
2 cups chicken broth
Stir in and blend until smooth: **2 cups dry white wine**

Pour mixture over meat in casserole.

Add to casserole: **8 cloves garlic, finely minced**
1 cup finely chopped parsley
1 cup finely chopped celery
2 cups chopped green pepper
2 cups chopped scallions
1 t. dry thyme
1 bay leaf
salt and pepper to taste

Cover. Simmer until meat is tender. To avoid last minute bustle, you may prepare meat and put it into casserole. Follow all steps up to adding white wine. At this point, you can wash skillet and put it away. Prepare vegetables, cover and set aside. One-half hour before serving, add wine, prepared vegetables, seasoning, and simmer.

MARINATED VEAL CHOPS—M

Serves six.

Marinate: **12 1 1/2-inch thick veal chops**
In mixture of: **1 cup cider vinegar**
1/2 cup salad oil
1/2 cup ketchup
1 onion, minced
1 clove garlic, sliced
1/2 t. ground thyme
1/2 t. chili powder
1/4 t. cayenne
1 T. salt

Broil slowly over charcoal or under medium broiler flame until brown on both sides, basting with left-over marinade.

VEAL SAUTÉED WITH WHITE WINE—M

Serves six.

In large skillet heat: **3 T. margarine**
Add and sauté: **1 lb. fresh mushrooms, sliced**

Remove mushrooms from skillet and arrange on oven-proof platter.

Add to skillet and heat: **6 T. margarine**
Add and brown: **3 lbs. veal, cut in strips, pounded thin, dredged in flour, seasoned with salt and pepper**
Add: **1/2 cup white wine**

Cook one minute longer. Transfer meat to center of oven-proof platter.

Add to skillet: **1/2 cup broth**

Scrape loose all brown particles and bring to boil. Pour over veal. Place platter in 350° oven for half hour. Garnish with parsley. You may prepare veal early in day, but don't place it in oven until one-half hour before ready to serve.

CROWN LAMB ROAST—M

Serves eight.

Have butcher prepare a crown roast with rib sections of lamb by tying two sections together in crown shape. Preheat oven to 350°. Cover tips of bones with aluminum foil to prevent charring. Place meat in roasting pan. Fill center with hamburg mixture.

Hamburg

Mix together:	**2 lbs. ground beef**
	1 egg
	1/4 cup water
	1/2 bottle Italian salad dressing
	1 t. salt

Bake at 350° for 1 1/2 hours. Remove aluminum foil and replace with paper frills.

LAMB-KA-BOBS—M

Six servings.

Cut lamb shoulder into 2 inch cubes and marinate overnight in refrigerator in:	**1 cup red wine**
	1/4 cup olive oil
	2 cloves garlic, crushed
	1 T. salt
	freshly ground black pepper
	1 t. orégano
Thread meat on skewers alternating with:	**mushroom caps**
	cherry tomatoes
	green pepper slices
	small white onions
	egg plant cubes

Brush with marinade. Cook over charcoal or broil under high heat, five minutes on each side.

POULTRY

CHICKEN BREASTS IN ROSÉ WINE—M

Serves six.

Brush: **3 whole breasts of chicken, halved**
With mixture of: **1/4 cup rosé wine**
2 T. melted margarine
2 t. lemon juice

Roast at 450° for 1/2 hour. Reduce heat to 350° and roast 1 hour more, basting once or twice. When browned and tender, arrange on heated platter and pour Rosé Sauce over chicken.

Rosé Sauce

In sauce pan, combine: **1 T. margarine**
1/2 cup currant jelly
1 T. lemon juice
3 whole cloves
dash cayenne
1/2 cup water
Simmer 5 minutes. Strain. Add: **1/2 cup rosé wine**
pan juices
Thicken with: **4 t. cornstarch**

CHICKEN CHASSEUR—M

Serves four.

Dredge: **1 2 1/2–3-lb. broiler, cut into pieces**
In mixture of: **flour**
salt
freshly ground black pepper
1/4 t. ground thyme

In large skillet, heat: **1/4 cup margarine**
Add and brown on all sides: **the chicken**
Add: **1/4 cup chopped shallots**
1/4 lb. chopped mushrooms
1/2 cup white wine
3/4 cup canned tomatoes
2 T. chopped parsley
1/4 t. tarragon

Cover and cook slowly until chicken is tender, 30–45 minutes.

CHICKEN AND CHERRIES—M

Serves six.

Dredge: **3 whole chicken breasts, halved**
In mixture of: **1/3 cup flour**
1 1/2 t. salt
1/4 t. garlic salt
1/2 t. paprika
Heat in skillet: **1/4 cup margarine**

Brown chicken slowly, turning once.

Add: **1 1–lb. can pitted, dark sweet cherries, drained**
Pour over all: **1 cup white wine**

Cover and cook slowly until chicken is tender, 30–45 minutes. When ready to serve, arrange in chafing dish. Place some of the cooked cherries over and around the chicken. Serve remaining sauce separately.

CHINESE CHICKEN—M

Serves six.

In skillet, heat: **2 T. vegetable oil**
Add and brown on all sides: **2 fryers, cut into serving pieces**

Drain off some oil and add to pan: **1/4 onion, chopped**
1/2 green pepper, cut in strips

Cook until onions are transparent.

Mix together and add: **1 cup pineapple syrup**
1 T. cornstarch
2 T. soy sauce
2 T. vinegar

Cook until clear and thickened.

Add and cook 5 minutes: **2 tomatoes, cut in chunks**
drained pineapple chunks

Serve in chafing dish with white rice.

CHINESE FRIED CHICKEN—M

Serves four.

Marinate for 30 minutes: **2 fryers, cut into eighths**
Marinade: **4 T. light soy sauce**
1/2 t. sesame oil
2 t. salt
2 T. gin or vodka

Drain chicken and discard marinade.

In bowl, beat until frothy: **4 egg whites**

Dip chicken in egg white.

On sheet of foil, place: **2 cups water-chestnut flour**

Coat chicken with flour.

In skillet, heat to 350°: **2 1/2 cups peanut oil**

Drop pieces of chicken into oil and cook until golden brown. Turn and fry until other side is golden brown. It is a good idea to add all white

or all dark pieces at a time, because the white chickens cooks faster than the dark. Fry all the chicken until brown and place on baking sheet and heat in oven at 350° until ready to serve.
(Optional) Chicken may be boned before marinating and served with Lemon Sauce.

CHICKEN IN CRUMBS—M

Serves six.

Melt:	**3/4 cup vegetable shortening**
In hot shortening, dip:	**2 broilers cut into serving pieces**
Dredge chicken in:	**1 box crushed crackers**

Place on shallow baking pan and bake at 350°, turning once.

CHICKEN CURRY—M

Serves four.

In a baking dish, place:	**2 fryers, quartered**
Dot with:	**2 T. margarine**
Sprinkle with:	**salt and pepper to taste**

Bake 15 minutes at 425°.

In a sauce pan, combine:	**1 1/2 cups orange juice**
	1/2 cup white raisins
	1/4 cup chopped chutney
	12 blanched almonds
	1/4 t. cinnamon
	1/4 t. curry

Simmer until blended and pour over chicken.
Reduce oven to 350° and bake for 1 hour.
To serve, you may garnish chicken with two sliced bananas and accompany the platter with small dishes of:

sliced scallions
crumbled beef fry
coconut

FRIED CHICKEN—M

Serves six.

Sprinkle with salt: **3 fryers cut into eighths**

In a large paper or plastic bag, place and shake until blended: **2 cups flour**
salt and pepper to taste
1 t. garlic powder
1 t. ground tarragon
1/4 t. thyme
1 t. paprika
1 t. onion powder

Add to bag a few pieces of the chicken at a time and shake until well coated. Place bag of chicken in refrigerator and chill until ready to fry.

In large skillet, heat to 375°: **2 1/2 cups of oil**

Drop pieces of chicken into oil and cook until golden brown. Turn and cook until other side is golden brown. It's a good idea to add all white or all dark pieces at a time, because the white chicken cooks faster than the dark. You can fry chicken until browned and place it on a baking sheet and heat in the oven (350°) until ready to serve.

CHICKEN WITH FRUIT MEDLEY—M

Serves six.

Sprinkle with salt: **3 fryers, cut in eighths**

In a bowl, mix: **2 eggs**
1 T. water

Dip chicken pieces into egg mixture.

In large bag, paper or plastic, place and shake until blended:
2 cups unseasoned bread crumbs
salt and pepper
1 t. ginger

Add to bag a few pieces of chicken at a time and shake until well coated. Place bag of chicken in refrigerator and chill until ready to fry.

In large skillet, heat to 375°:
1 stick margarine
1/2 cup oil

Place pieces of chicken into heated oil and margarine and brown on both sides. At this point in the recipe, you may freeze the chicken and defrost and finish preparing when ready to serve.
Place chicken in baking dish and pour sauce over it.

Sauce

In sauce pan, combine:
1 T. cornstarch, dissolved in
1/4 cup cold water
1 T. brown sugar
2 T. ketchup
2 T. soy sauce
2 1/2 cups fruit juice, drained from:
1 large jar fruits for salad
1 large can apricots
1 large can pineapple chunks

Bring to the boil and cook until clear.
Pour sauce over chicken and garnish with fruits. Bake at 350° uncovered for 45 minutes.

CHICKEN IN GRAPES AND ORANGES—M

Serves six to eight.

Heat in skillet: **1/2 cup margarine**
Brown on both sides: **2 broilers, cut in quarters**
Return chicken to skillet and add: **1 1/2 cups orange juice**

2 T. slivered orange peel
2 t. onion, minced
1/4 t. ginger
1/4 t. Tabasco sauce

Simmer until chicken is tender, 30 minutes.
Arrange chicken on heated platter.

To thicken sauce in skillet, add: **4 t. cornstarch, blended with a little cold water**

Cook, stirring constantly until mixture thickens and comes to boil.

Add: **2 oranges, sectioned and peeled**
2 cups seedless grapes
1/2 cup toasted, slivered almonds

Pour sauce over chicken, and carefully and attractively arrange the orange sections and grapes around it.

HAWAIIAN CHICKEN—M

Serves six. A simple and delicious way to use cooked chicken.

In sauce pan, cook just till tender: **1 1/2 cups sliced celery**
1 green pepper, cut in strips
in
3 T margarine

Add: **3 cups cooked chicken, cubed**
1 22-oz. can pineapple pie filling
1/3 cup water
1/4 cup soy sauce
2 t. instant chicken bouillon powder

Cook and stir till hot. Serve over chow mein noodles and garnish with parsley and kumquats, if desired.

CHICKEN WITH HONEY AND MUSTARD—M

Serves six.

Sprinkle with salt and pepper: **3 fryers, cut in eighths**
In a bowl, combine: **1/4 lb. melted margarine**
1 5-oz. jar Dijon mustard
1/3 cup honey

Dip pieces of chicken into mixture and coat well.
Place on baking sheet and bake at 350° for 1 1/2 hours.

CHICKEN KIEV—M

Serves four.

Place between two pieces of waxed paper and pound until thin: **4 whole breasts of chicken, halved**

Do not split the flesh
Remove the waxed paper.

Cut into eight finger-shaped pieces and place in middle of each breast: **1 oz. chilled margarine**
Sprinkle with: **salt**
freshly ground black pepper
1 T. chopped chives
1 T. tarragon

Roll up breasts, being sure to seal the sides as you roll.
Dredge each roll lightly with flour.

Dip in: **2 eggs, lightly beaten**
Roll in: **1 1/3 cups fresh bread crumbs**

Refrigerate at least 1 hour, so that the crumbs will adhere. Fill deep fryer with enough fat to completely cover the breasts. Heat to 360° and add chicken. Brown on all sides.
Drain thoroughly on absorbent paper and serve.

CHICKEN A LA KING—M

Six servings.

Melt in sauce pan: **4 T. margarine**
Stir in: **4 T. flour**
Add: **2 cups clear chicken broth**

When sauce boils, blend 2 tablespoons of hot sauce with one egg yolk. Add mixture to sauce. Stir constantly.

When sauce thickens, add, and heat well: **3 cups cut-up cooked chicken**
1/3 cup canned pimento
2 cans mushrooms
3/4 cup slivered, blanched almonds
salt
white pepper
1 box frozen peas, defrosted
Just before serving, add: **1 jigger sherry**

Serve in acorn-squash or patty shells.

CHICKEN AND KUMQUATS—M

Serves six.

Sprinkle with salt and pepper: **3 fryers, cut in eighths**

Place skin side down in a baking dish.

In a bowl, combine: **1 cup orange juice**
2 T. fresh lemon juice
1/4 cup honey
2 T. chopped chili peppers

Pour mixture over chicken and bake at 375° for 15 minutes.

Turn pieces of chicken over and add: **10 preserved kumquats**

Baste occasionally and bake for another hour until the chicken is nicely browned.
To serve, arrange on platter, pour pan juices over chicken, and garnish with lemon or orange slices.

LIME-BROILED CHICKEN—M

Serves four.

Place skin side up on rack 6 inches from broiler heat:	**1 broiler, cut in serving pieces**
Brush with sauce of:	**1/4 cup corn oil**
	1/4 cup lime juice
	1 T. chopped onion
	1 t. tarragon
	1 t. salt
	freshly ground black pepper
	1/4 t. Tabasco sauce

Broil slowly until tender, turning and basting occasionally 1–1 1/4 hours. May be baked in oven at 350° for 1–1 1/4 hours.

CHICKEN IN PINEAPPLE BOATS—M

Serves six.

Melt in large sauce pan:	**1/4 cup shortening**
Add:	**2 small onions, chopped**
	1 clove garlic, minced
	1 stalk celery
	1 tart apple, diced

Cook for 8 minutes, stirring occasionally.

Stir in:	**1/4 cup flour**
	2 t. curry powder
	1 t. salt
	1/2 t. dry mustard

Cook for 2 minutes, stirring.

Add: **1 bay leaf**
2 cups chicken broth

Stir until sauce thickens. Simmer 30 minutes.

Add: **3 cups cooked chicken**
1/2 cup milk substitute (optional)
2 T. chutney
1 cup diced fresh pineapple

Cool.

Cut in half lengthwise and scoop out: **3 small pineapples**

Fill shells with chicken mixture. Top with shredded coconut.
When ready to serve, arrange on baking dish and bake at 350° until well heated, about 15 minutes.

CHICKEN IN RICE—M

Serves six.

Heat in skillet: **1/4 cup olive oil**
Brown on both sides: **1 4-lb. frying chicken, cut in serving pieces**
Seasoned with: **1 1/2 t. salt**
1/2 t. pepper
1/8 t. paprika

Remove chicken to casserole.

To skillet add and sauté: **1 clove garlic, minced**
1 medium onion, chopped
2 cups clear chicken broth
3 1/2 cups canned whole tomatoes
1/4 t. powdered saffron
1 bay leaf
1/2 t. orégano
1/2 t. salt

Bring to boil and pour over chicken.

Add: **2 cups raw rice**

Stir and cover tightly. Bake 25 minutes at 350°, uncover and toss the rice.

Stir in: **1/2 pkg. frozen peas, defrosted**
1/2 pkg. artichoke hearts, defrosted
Arrange on top: **3 pimentoes, cut in pieces**

Cover and cook 10 minutes longer.

CHICKEN SALAD—M

Serves six.

Combine and chill: **4 cups cooked chicken, diced**
2 cups celery, diced
1 cup whole blanched almonds
1 cup canned pineapple chunks, well drained
1 t. salt
freshly ground black pepper
1 cup mayonnaise
1/4 t. Tabasco sauce

Garnish with pimento and serve on lettuce cups.

SHERRIED CHICKEN ON GREEN NOODLES—M

Serves six to eight.

Place in heavy kettle: **2 broilers cut into serving pieces**
Cover with: **3 cups clear chicken broth**

Bring to boil. Simmer covered until meat can be removed from bones, 30–40 minutes. Remove chicken.

In sauce pan, melt: **6 T. margarine**
Add and stir with wire whisk: **6 T. flour**

Add boiling broth. Stir until sauce is thickened and smooth.

Season with: **salt**
freshly ground black pepper
1/2 t. paprika

Stir in: **1/4 cup sherry**

Remove meat from chicken bones and add to sauce.

Add: **1 small can mushrooms**

Serve on Green Spinach Noodles, cooked according to package directions. When noodles are drained, return to cooking pot and add 1 tablespoon margarine to keep noodles from sticking until serving time.

CHICKEN IN SWEET AND SOUR SAUCE—M

Serves six.

Place in shallow baking dish and dot with margarine: **2 broilers, cut in serving pieces**

Season with: **salt**
pepper

Bake at 350° for 3/4 hour.

Pour over chicken a sauce of: **1 8-oz. jar sweet and sour sauce**
3 T. brown sugar
3 T. sherry
1/3 cup orange juice

Bake for 3/4 hour more. Baste occasionally.

COQ AU VIN—M

Serves six.

Dredge in flour: **1 5-lb. roasting chicken, cut into serving pieces**

In skillet, heat: **1/2 cup margarine**

Add chicken and brown on all sides.

Remove chicken to casserole and add:	**10 small, whole, white onions, peeled**
	1 clove garlic, finely chopped
	1/2 t. tarragon
	1 t. parsley, chopped
	1 bay leaf
	10 whole mushrooms
	salt
	freshly ground black pepper, to taste
Pour over chicken and ignite:	**1/4 cup warmed cognac**
When flame dies, add:	**1 cup dry red wine**

Cover and bake until chicken is tender, about 2 1/2 hours.

COQ AU VIN #2—M

Serves six.

In a skillet, heat:	**1/4 cup oil**
Brown:	**1 5-lb. roasting chicken, cut into serving pieces**
Add:	**1/2 cup warmed cognac**
	3/4 bottle red wine

Heat for a few minutes to allow liquid to boil down.

Remove chicken to casserole and add:	**1 bay leaf**
	1/4 t. thyme
	10 whole fresh mushrooms
	10 small whole white onions, peeled

Cover and bake at 350° for 2 hours, until chicken is tender.

DUCK À L'ORANGE—M

Serves four.

On a rack on shallow roasting pan, place:	**2 5-lb. ducklings**
Rub cavities with:	**lemon juice**
Place in each cavity:	**1 whole onion**
	1 leek

Roast at 325° for one-half hour. Drain fat from pan.

Add:	**2 cups white wine**

Baste ducks every 20 minutes and cook for 1 1/2 hours.

Fifteen minutes before finishing, baste with:	**2 T. honey**
	1 cup chilled white wine

Skim off all fat.

Place remaining juices in sauce pan and add:	**4 T. margarine**

grated rind of 2 oranges

1 cup mushrooms, sliced

2 small cloves garlic, crushed

Bring mixture to boil and simmer 2 minutes. Remove pan from heat and

Blend in:	**6 T. flour**
Stir in:	**1/2 cup sherry**
	1/2 cup brandy
	1/2 cup Cointreau
	1/2 cup orange juice

Return pan to heat and stir mixture until smooth and thick.

Add:	**2 T. currant jelly**
Remove garlic and season with:	**salt and pepper to taste**

May be refrigerated. When ready to serve, cut ducks in quarters, reheat in sauce, thoroughly. Arrange on serving platter. Pour over sauce and garnish with slices of orange.

ROCK CORNISH HEN—M

Four hens serve four.

Place in shallow casserole: **4 rock cornish hens, stuffed and tied**

Stuffing

Brown in margarine: **1 small onion, diced**
Add and cook 5 minutes: **1/3 cup mushrooms, diced**
Add and mix well: **3/4 cup wild rice, cooked**

Bake at 350° for 1 hour or until tender. Baste often with margarine. Serve with Cherry Orange Sauce.

STUFFED TURKEY—M

Serves ten.

Rub salt into inner cavity of: **1 12-lb. turkey**

Fill with stuffing, skewer, tie, wrap with aluminum foil and roast at 400° for 4 hours. Remove foil for last 1/2 hour to brown.

Stuffing

Combine in mixing bowl:
1 box crackers, crushed
2 cups corn flakes, crushed
2 T. turkey fat, in pieces
1 large onion, grated
1 carrot, grated
1 small potato, grated
1 stalk celery, grated
dash salt
freshly ground pepper to taste
garlic salt to taste

Serve with mushroom gravy.

STUFFED TURKEY #2—M

Serves ten.

Prepare turkey as in preceding recipe but do not use tin foil. Rub skin with margarine. Place turkey in large paper bag and roast at 325°, 20 minutes per pound. Open bag last 20 minutes to make sure turkey is well browned.

FISH

FISH CHASSEUR—D

Serves four.

Place in greased shallow baking dish:	**2 lbs. fish filets**
Dot with:	**2 T. butter**

Pour sauce over fish and bake at 350° for 20 minutes.

Sauce

In sauce pan, melt:	**1/4 cup butter**
Add and sauté:	**1 onion, sliced**
	1/2 green pepper, diced
Add and cook 10 minutes:	**1/2 cup celery, diced**
	1 bay leaf
	salt
	freshly ground black pepper
	1 medium can tomatoes
	1/4 cup ketchup
	1/2 t. basil
	1 T. sugar

FISH CRÊPES

2 1/2 dozen.

Crêpes—D

In bowl, beat with wire whisk:	**4 eggs**
Add and beat until smooth:	**1 cup flour**
	2 T. sugar
	1 T. parsley
	1 T. tarragon
	1 T. chives
Add gradually and stir until smooth:	**2 cups milk**

For method, see Dessert Crêpe for Crêpes Suzette.

Filling

Cook for 10 minutes:	**1 lb. haddock filet**
	2 cups water
	1 carrot
	1 onion
	salt and pepper

Remove fish from water and reserve water.

In a sauce pan, combine:	**cooked fish**
	1 T. finely chopped shallots
	1/2 cup dry white wine

Bring to boil and cook until wine is reduced by half.

In another sauce pan, melt, mixing constantly:	**1/4 cup margarine**
	1/2 cup flour
Stir in and cook until slightly thick:	**2 cups fish stock**

Fold fish mixture into thickened stock.

Add:	**1 t. finely chopped parsley**
	1/2 t. chopped tarragon
	1/2 t. chopped chives

Remove sauce pan from heat and add:	**3 egg yolks beaten with**
	1/2 cup of milk
	2 t. anise seed
	1 t. lemon juice
	salt
Fold in:	**1/2 cup heavy cream**

Fill crêpe, fold it over, and place in baking dish. Spoon remaining fish mixture over crêpes and bake at 400° for 15 minutes. Garnish with seedless green grapes.

For additional fish crêpes, see Appetizers.

FRIED FISH, ENGLISH STYLE—D

Serves four.

In a bowl, place:	**1 cup flour**
Make a well and add:	**1 egg yolk**
	2 T. beer
	1/4 t. salt

Mix well together.

Gradually stir in:	**3 T. milk**
	3 T. water
In small bowl, beat until frothy:	**1 egg white**

Fold egg white into mixture.
Place fish in mixture and coat each piece well.

In skillet, heat to 400°:	**2 cups oil**

Fry fish a few pieces at a time until brown on one side. When brown, carefully turn and brown other side. Do not crowd pan. You may fry the fish ahead and place on baking sheet. Heat at 350° for 10 minutes when ready to serve.

FISH MOUSSE—D

Serves four.

In blender, place: **1 lb. fish using combination of:**
sole
white fish
pike
2 cups cream
2 egg whites
salt

Blend well. Pour into buttered Charlotte Russe. Cover with buttered tin foil. Set mousse pan in pan of hot water to a depth of 1 inch, and bake for 20 minutes at 350°. Unmold and serve with Champagne Sauce.

Champagne Sauce

In a sauce pan, heat: **3 T. butter**
Add, stirring constantly: **3 T. flour**

Beat well with wire whisk.

Gradually stir in: **1 cup fish stock, warmed**

Let it come to the boil and thicken, stirring constantly.

Remove from heat and add: **1/2 cup champagne**

FISH SALAD—P

Serves six.

In sauce pan, place: **2 lbs. fish filets**
water to cover
1 stalk celery
carrot
onion
peppercorn
bay leaf
1 t. salt

Cook until fish flakes with fork, about 15 minutes.
Remove from pan, reserving some of fish stock.

Combine in bowl: **flaked fish**
2 stalks celery, diced
2 t. grated onion
1 T. sliced pimento
1 t. celery seed
salt
freshly ground pepper
1/4 cup fish stock
1/4 cup diced green pepper
1/2 cup mayonnaise
2 T. lemon juice

Toss gently and chill. For dairy, serve on lettuce cups with Frozen Horseradish Squares.

FISH STOCK—P

One quart.

In sauce pan, heat: **1 T. margarine**
Add: **1 lb. fish bones**
6 cups water

Cook, stirring, for about 5 minutes.

Add: **1/4 t. thyme**
1 bay leaf
1 clove garlic
1 onion, coarsely chopped
4 peppercorns
1 large carrot, chopped
1/2 cup leeks, chopped
1 stalk celery with leaves
1 t. salt
1/4 cup parsley

Bring to the boil. Simmer 30 minutes and strain. May be frozen and defrosted as needed or may be kept in refrigerator for one week.

ROLLED STUFFED FISH—D

Serves four.

In skillet, heat:	**2 T. butter**
Sauté:	**2/3 cup celery, finely chopped**
	1 large onion, finely chopped
	1/4 lb. fresh mushrooms, chopped
Add:	**1 large can red salmon**
	1/2 cup bread crumbs
	salt
	freshly ground pepper
	1 T. lemon juice
	1/4 t. dill
	1/2 t. allspice
	1 egg, slightly beaten
Spread mixture on:	**8 thin flounder or sole filets**

Roll up and place in lightly greased baking dish. Dot with butter. Bake at 350° 20–30 minutes. Serve with White Sauce with green grapes.

BAKED HADDOCK—D

Serves four.

In small skillet, melt:	**1/4 lb. butter**
Add and mix together:	**1 t. Worcestershire sauce**
	1/2 t. garlic powder
In this mixture, dip:	**2 lbs. haddock filets**

Place fish in lightly greased baking dish.

Pour over fish:	**1 can cream of mushroom soup**
	1 can milk

Bake at 375° for 30 minutes.

In a bowl, mix:	**16 crackers, crushed**
	3 T. butter
	2 T. chopped onion

Spread cracker mixture over baked fish.
Bake 10 minutes longer.

FLAKED HADDOCK, REMOULADE—P

Serves six.

Cook as for Fish Salad. Flake, chill and serve on lettuce cups with Remoulade Sauce.

KIPPERED HERRING—P

Serves six.

Place in shallow baking dish, skin side up:	**3 kippers, split in half**
Dot with:	**margarine**

Heat thoroughly at 350° for 20 minutes. When ready to serve, sprinkle with chopped chives and serve with wedges of lemon.

COLD SALMON—P

Serves eight.

Boil together for one-half hour:	**3 lbs. fresh salmon**
	1 onion
	2 stalks celery
	1 cup water
	1/4 t. salt
	peppercorns
	1 carrot, whole
	1/4 cup vinegar

Cool and remove fish carefully. Serve with Salmon Sauce.

SALMON QUICHE—D

Serves six.

Partially bake:	**1 9-inch pastry shell (see Index)**
In small skillet, heat:	**2 T. butter**
Sauté:	**2 T. minced shallots**
Drain, skin, and reserve 1/4 cup liquid from:	**1 1-lb. can red salmon**
In electric blender, blend for 20 seconds:	**shallots**
	salmon
	2 T. snipped dill
	4 eggs
	salmon liquid
	2 T. sherry
	1/8 t. pepper
Turn blender to low speed and add:	**1 cup heavy cream, scalded**

Pour into pastry shell and bake 25–35 minutes at 375° until Quiche is puffed and brown.

SALMON TOAST CUPS—D

Serves six.

Combine in bowl:	**1 large can red salmon**
	1 T. lemon juice
	1 T. grated onion
	salt
	paprika
	freshly ground black pepper
	1 cup finely diced celery
	1/2 cup mayonnaise

Divide mixture into 12 toast cups.

Toast Cups

Trim crusts: **12 slices white bread**

Roll each slice thin with rolling pin. Spread with melted butter. Press into muffin cups. Toast slightly in 350° oven for 5 minutes. Fill cups with mixture and return to oven for 20 minutes.
Toast cups may be filled with Tuna Salad or Cheese mixture as given for Cheese Roll-Ups

ROLLED FILET OF SOLE—D

Serves four to six.

Butter well the bottom of a heavy shallow baking pan (about 3-quart).

Sprinkle with: **10 chopped shallots**
salt and pepper

Cut into lengthwise strips: **8 filets of sole (2 lbs.)**

Roll each strip into a tight cylinder lengthwise, starting at the small end. Place fish rolls upright in the prepared pan. If you place them close together, they will not unroll.

Sprinkle fish with: **10 more chopped shallots**
salt and pepper

Add: **1 large (1 lb. 12-oz.) can tomatoes, chopped**
1/2 cup parsley, minced
1 1/2 cups dry white wine mixed with 1 cup water

Cover fish with piece of buttered waxed paper or tin foil. Place pan over high heat and bring to boil. Place pan in preheated 400° oven for 10–12 minutes. Remove from oven and transfer fish rolls to buttered serving platter. Cover again with buttered paper and keep warm.
Pour liquid from baking pan into a sauce pan. Bring to rolling boil and reduce until you have two-thirds left.

In small skillet, melt: **3 T. butter**

Add, stirring constantly: **3 T. flour**

Add butter-flour roux to the liquid, whipping constantly with a wire whisk. Cook until lightly thickened, stirring constantly.

Add: **3/4 cup heavy cream**

Bring to the boil. Remove from heat.

In small bowl, beat: **3 egg yolks**
1/4 cup heavy cream

Combine with hot liquid, whipping constantly.

Add: **2 T. cognac**
Beat in: **4 T. butter**

Pour sauce over filets and sprinkle with: 1/2 cup parsley, minced

SWORDFISH KA-BOBS—D

Serves four.

Cut into cubes: **1 1/2 lbs. swordfish**
Marinate for 2 hours in: **1 clove garlic, minced**
1/4 cup finely chopped parsley
1/4 cup lemon juice
2/3 cup peanut oil
salt
freshly ground black pepper
1/2 t. thyme
3 drops Tabasco sauce

Thread skewers with alternate pieces of: **swordfish**
1 can small round onions
pieces of green pepper
cherry tomatoes
artichoke hearts

Brush skewers with marinade sauce. Place over charcoal or under broiler, turning once until fish flakes easily.

Pass bowl of: **1 stick butter, melted**
juice of 1/2 lemon

TUNA SALAD WITH APPLES—P

Serves four.

Combine in bowl:
2 cans tuna fish
2 medium green apples, diced but not peeled
1/2 cup celery, diced
1/2 cup walnuts, chopped
1 t. salt
white pepper to taste
1/2 cup Italian salad dressing

Toss and serve on lettuce cups garnished with hard-boiled egg slices, unpeeled cucumber slices, and green stuffed-olive slices.

LASAGNA LENORA—D

Serves twelve.

Noodles

In large sauce pan, cook and drain according to package directions:
1 box Lasagna noodles with
1 t. olive oil

Sauce

In skillet heat:
2 T. olive oil

Add and simmer:
1 large can Italian tomatoes
1 can tomato paste
1 small can mushroom pieces

In blender, combine and blend:
1 small can mushroom pieces
1 onion, sliced
2 cloves garlic
1/4 t. rosemary
1/4 t. orégano
1/4 t. basil
salt

freshly ground black pepper
1 T. parsley flakes

When blended add to skillet.

Cheese

In bowl, combine and blend: **1 lb. Farmers' cheese**
1 egg, beaten
Add: **8 oz. Gruyère**
3 oz. Parmesan

In 9 × 13″ baking pan, place layer of sauce. Add layer of noodles, add a little more sauce, a layer of cheese. Alternate layers as described, ending with layer of sauce. Sprinkle with Parmesan cheese. Bake at 350°, one hour.

Starches

BARLEY PILAF—M

Serves ten.

In skillet, heat:	**1/2 cup margarine**
Sauté:	**1/2 lb. fresh mushrooms**
	1/2 cup onion, chopped
Add and cook until brown:	**1–1/3 cups pearl barley**

Remove from heat and turn into 2-qt. casserole.

Add:	**2 cups clear chicken broth**

Bake covered 30 minutes at 350°.

Stir in:	**2 more cups chicken broth**

Bake 30 minutes more.

Stir in:	**1 more cup chicken broth**

Bake 20 minutes more, uncovered.

GARLIC BREAD—P

Serves six.

Cut in 1 1/2″ slices but not quite through to bottom:	**1 loaf French bread**
Brush each cut side with:	**1/4 lb. melted margarine**
	1 t. garlic juice
	2 T. parsley, chopped

Brush top with remaining melted margarine mixture and sprinkle with additional chopped parsley.
Wrap loaf in aluminum foil. Refrigerate until ready to use. When ready to serve, bake at 400°, 15–20 minutes.

POPPY SEED NOODLES—P

Serves eight or ten.

Cook and drain according to directions on package:	**1 1-lb. box wide noodles**
Return noodles to pot and stir in:	**1/2 cup poppy seeds**
	1 t. salt
In small skillet, heat:	**1 cup margarine**
Add and sauté until golden:	**1 1/2 cups slivered blanched almonds**

Add to noodles.

NOODLE PUDDING

Serves twelve.

Cook and drain according to directions on box:	**1 lb. wide noodles**

Return noodles to pot and mix with desired combination of ingredients. Place in well-greased 9 × 13″ baking dish and bake at 350° 1 hour.

Combinations: #1.—**M**

6 eggs, well beaten
2 T. chicken fat
2 T. salt or to taste
freshly ground black pepper
1 t. cinnamon
2 T. sugar
1/2 cup white raisins and/or 1/2 cup peeled, diced apple
Before placing in oven, sprinkle top with additional cinnamon.

#2.—**P**

6 eggs, well beaten
1 stick melted margarine
1 cup apple sauce
1 1/2 lbs. apples, peeled and diced
3/4 cup sugar
2 t. vanilla
1/2 box white raisins
salt and pepper to taste
Before placing in oven, dribble 1/2 stick additional melted margarine over top.

#3.—**P**

6 eggs, well beaten
1 stick melted margarine
1 medium can fruit cocktail, drained. Reserve cherries.
salt and pepper to taste
1 T. sugar (optional)
Before placing in oven, sprinkle top with crushed cornflakes and place reserved cherries.

#4.—**P**

6 eggs, well beaten
6 T. chopped scallions
2 cups cooked spinach, chopped
1 T. salt
1 stick melted margarine

#5.—**D**

6 eggs, well beaten
1 pt. sour cream
1/2 lb. cottage cheese
1/4 lb. cream cheese
3 T. melted butter
2 T. sugar
1 t. cinnamon
salt and pepper to taste
1/2 box white raisins
Before placing in oven, sprinkle with bread crumbs and dot with butter.

#6.—**D**

6 eggs, well beaten
1 pt. sour cream
1/2 lb. cream cheese
3 T. melted butter
salt and pepper to taste
1 medium can crushed pineapple, well drained
Sprinkle with crushed corn flakes and dot with butter.
Blend in electric blender:

#7.—**D**

6 eggs, well beaten
1/2 lb. cream cheese
1/2 lb. cottage cheese
3/4 cup milk
1 cup sugar
6 slices American cheese
1 pt. sour cream
1 t. vanilla
salt and pepper to taste
1/2 stick melted butter
1/2 box white raisins
Sprinkle with bread crumbs and 1/2 stick melted butter.

GERMAN PANCAKES—D

Serves four.

Pre-heat oven to 450°.

In a bowl, beat until light:	**3 eggs**
Add:	**1/2 t. salt**
	1/2 cup flour
Mix well and add:	**1/2 cup milk**
	2 T. butter

Spread bottom and sides of 10-inch skillet with butter. Pour in batter and bake for 20 minutes. Reduce heat to 350° and bake until crisp and brown. Serve with confectioner's sugar and lemon wedges.

Apple variation

Add to batter 1/2 cup peeled and diced apples seasoned with 1 tablespoon sugar and 1/2 teaspoon cinnamon.

POPOVERS—P

Eight servings.

Pre-heat oven to 425°.

Place in bowl and beat with rotary beater until very smooth:	**1 cup all-purpose flour**
	1/2 t. salt
	2 eggs
	1 cup milk substitute
	1 T. salad oil

Fill greased aluminum popover pans a little less than one-half full. Bake, without peeking, about 35 minutes or until sides are firm. Serve immediately.

BAKED STUFFED POTATOES

Serves eight.

Bake at 400° 1 hour and cool: **8 large baking potatoes, wrapped in foil**

Slice thin layer off top and scoop out.

#1.-**P** beat in electric mixer at medium speed:
potatoes
1/4 lb. margarine
2 eggs
1 T. salt
pepper to taste
2 T. parsley flakes

Refill potato shells, heaping full. May be refrigerated. When ready to serve, sprinkle with paprika. Brown in 400° oven until hot.

#2.-**D** beat in electric mixer at medium speed:
potatoes
1 cup sour cream
1/2 cup chopped chives
1/2 t. nutmeg
1 egg
salt
pepper to taste

Finish as above.

FRENCH-FRIED POTATOES—P

Allow one potato per person, three per teenager.

Peel, pare, and slice into 3/8-inch strips: **Potatoes**

Place in bowl of cold water and keep changing the water until it is clear. Drain water and pat potatoes dry with a paper towel.

Heat to 400° in deep heavy pot: **1 large (38-oz.) bottle oil**

Throw the potatoes in the pre-heated oil. Do not stir until they are well browned. Remove from heat and place on tray lined with paper toweling to absorb oil. If you have too many potatoes for one batch, allow the oil to return to original temperature. When all potatoes are done and you are ready to serve, place them all back into the hot oil for few minutes and serve. You may put them in the oven for a few minutes, being careful that they do not dry out.

OVEN-FRIED POTATOES—P

Serves six.

In shallow baking dish, place:	**2 lbs. potatoes, peeled and sliced**
	2 onions, sliced thin
	1 t. chopped parsley
	1 t. salt
	pepper to taste
Dot with:	**3 T. vegetable shortening**
Add:	**1 cup boiling water**
Sprinkle with:	**paprika**

Bake 400°, 40 minutes or until brown and crusty on top and water is absorbed.

POTATO PUDDING—M

Serves six to eight.

Combine in bowl:	**3 eggs, beaten until thick**
	3 cups grated, drained potatoes
	1/3 cup flour
	1/2 t. baking powder
	1 1/2 t. salt
	1/8 t. pepper
	3 T. grated onion
	4 T. melted chicken fat

Into 1 1/2-quart baking dish, put enough oil to fill baking dish one-eighth full. Heat until 1/8 teaspoon of batter sizzles when dropped into oil, about 15 minutes.
Drop potato mixture into hot oil. Bake at 400° for one hour. Serve immediately. May be made in muffin cups.

CANDIED SWEET POTATOES—P

Serves six to eight.

In shallow baking dish lined with aluminum foil, place:	**6 sweet potatoes, partly cooked, peeled, halved**
In sauce pan, boil together for 10 minutes:	**2 cups dark brown sugar**
	1 cup boiling water
Add:	**1/2 t. salt**
	1/2 t. cinnamon
	1 T. margarine

Pour hot sauce over potatoes. Bake at 350° 45 minutes until potatoes are tender, basting occasionally.
Same recipe may be followed and topped with marshmallows cut in half and browned.

SWEET POTATOES IN ORANGE BASKETS—P

Serves ten.

With sharp paring knife, cut off slice from top and scoop out pulp of:	**10 seedless oranges**

Fill with sweet potato filling.

Combine:	**3 cups cooked sweet potatoes, mashed**
	2 T. margarine

1/2 t. salt
1/2 t. grated lemon rind
2 eggs, well beaten
molasses to taste
1/2 t. cinnamon
1/4 t. cloves
1/4 t. ginger
3/4 cup crushed pineapple, drained

Bake at 350° 20–25 minutes. Serve immediately garnished with sections of the scooped-out orange.

VIENNESE POTATOES—M

Serves four.

Boil with their skins on for 10 minutes: **3 potatoes (large)**

Cool slightly. Peel and cut lengthwise into slices about 1/2 inch thick.

In large skillet, melt: **2 T. margarine**
Add: **1/4 cup finely chopped onions**

Cook about 8 minutes over medium heat until they are lightly colored.

Stir in and mix until thoroughly absorbed: **1 1/2 tablespoons flour**
Reduce heat to low and stir in with wire whisk: **1 1/4 cups beef stock**
Add: **1/2 t. capers**
1 t. grated lemon peel
1/8 t. marjoram
1/2 t. salt
freshly ground pepper
1/8 t. thyme
1 small bay leaf
2 T. finely chopped sour pickles

Bring sauce to boil and add: **potatoes**
1 T. white vinegar

Cover skillet and simmer about 25 minutes, until tender. Remove bay leaf and garnish with parsley before serving.

FRIED RICE—P

Serves eight to ten.

In skillet, heat: **3 t. peanut oil**
Swish in mixture of: **2 eggs**
1/4 cup water
1 t. cornstarch
Add: **1 1/4 cups cooked white rice**
8 mushrooms, chopped
8 water chestnuts, chopped
3 pimentoes, chopped
1 large onion, chopped
1 can bamboo shoots, drained
3 T. soy sauce
1/2 t. salt

Stir and fry 6 minutes.

RISOTTO D'ANGELO—M

Serves six or eight.

In large skillet, heat: **1/4 lb. margarine**
Sauté until brown: **1/2 cup crushed thin noodles**
Add: **2 cups uncooked rice, rinsed**
1 T. allspice
salt
4 1/2 cups clear chicken broth

Cook on slow heat for 20 minutes.

RICE PILAF—M

Serves six.

In skillet, melt:	**1/4 cup margarine**
Add:	**1/2 cup chopped green pepper**
	1 cup uncooked rice

Brown 6–8 minutes.

Add:	**1 can onion soup**
	1/2 cup water
	dash of pepper
	salt

Cover and simmer 30 minutes until liquid is gone.

SPANISH RICE—P

Serves six or eight.

In large skillet, heat:	**1/4 lb. margarine**
Add and sauté:	**1 large onion, chopped**
	1 green pepper, chopped
	1 clove garlic, chopped
	1/4 lb. fresh mushrooms, chopped
Add and bring to boil:	**3 cups canned tomatoes**
	1 can tomato sauce
	1 bay leaf
	2 drops Tabasco sauce
	1 T. sugar
	salt
	freshly ground black pepper
	1 t. basil
Add:	**2 cups uncooked rice**

Simmer for 20 minutes.

RICE STRAUSS—M

Serves four to six.

In skillet, melt: **1/4 cup margarine**
Add and brown: **1 cup uncooked rice**
1 large onion, chopped
Remove from heat and add: **1 1/2 cans clear chicken broth**
1/2 cup shredded coconut
1/2 cup slivered almonds
1 can sliced mushrooms

Put in casserole. Bake at 350° for 40 minutes.

WILD RICE RING—M

Serves four.

In large sauce pan, heat: **1 T. margarine**
Add and sauté: **2 scallions, chopped**
Add: **1 cup wild rice, washed thoroughly**
1 t. salt
2 cups clear chicken broth

Bring to boil, stir once and reduce heat. Cover tightly and cook until rice is tender and liquid is absorbed, about 35 minutes.

In large skillet, heat: **2 T. peanut oil**
Add and sauté 5 minutes: **4 large mushrooms, chopped**
1 4-oz. can water chestnuts, drained and chopped
1/4 cup toasted almonds
Remove from heat and combine: **the cooked wild rice**
mushroom-nut mixture
1 cup white rice, cooked
salt and pepper to taste

Spoon mixture into greased 7-inch ring mold. Keep hot in very slow oven until ready to serve. Unmold and transfer to heated platter. Fill center with 2 cups cooked fresh peas.

YORKSHIRE PUDDING—M

Serves four.

Preheat oven to 450°.

In a bowl, beat:	**2 eggs** **1 cup beef stock**
Stir in:	**1 cup flour** **1/2 t. salt**

Beat until well blended.

Place in 11 × 7″ baking pan:	**drippings from roast beef** **enough oil to make 1/4 cup combined**

Heat in oven for a few minutes.
Pour in pudding mixture and bake 10 minutes. Reduce oven temperature to 350° and bake 15–20 minutes longer until puffy and delicately browned. Cut into squares and serve immediately with roast beef.

Vegetables

ACORN SQUASH—P

Serves four.

Cut in half lengthwise and scoop out seeds and fibers of: **2 acorn squash**

Prick the flesh in several places with a fork. Place in baking pan cut side down. Bake 30 minutes at 375°.

Turn squash over and brush with mixture of:
1/4 cup melted margarine
1/4 cup corn syrup
1/2 t. salt

Bake 30 minutes longer. Baste frequently.

ASPARAGUS VINAIGRETTE—P

Serves four.

Cook and drain according to directions: **1 box frozen asparagus spears**

Pour Vinaigrette Sauce over hot or cold cooked asparagus and let stand 1 hour, turning the asparagus once.

BEAN SPROUTS—P

Serves four.

Rinse thoroughly:	**2 lbs. fresh bean sprouts**
Steam in sauce pan with:	**1/4 cup water**
	1 t. salt
	dash of sugar

Drain and serve.

HARVARD BEETS—P

Serves four to six.

In sauce pan, combine and heat until thick and smooth:	**1/3 cup sugar**
	2 t. cornstarch
	1/4 cup vinegar
	liquid from 1 can of beets
Add:	**1 1-lb. can beets, sliced**
	1 T. margarine

Heat through.

HAWAIIAN BEETS—P

Serves four to six.

In sauce pan, combine and heat:	**1 can small, round, whole beets**
	1 medium can pineapple chunks, drained

MAC

1/2 t. salt
2 t. vinegar
Combine: **2 t. cornstarch**
2 t. syrup from pineapple chunks

Add to sauce pan and heat until beets are glazed.

BROCCOLI MEDLEY—P

Serves four to six.

In wok or skillet heat: **1 T. oil**
Add: **1 medium onion, sliced**
1 bunch broccoli, sliced
1 head cauliflower, sliced
2 zucchini, sliced
1/2 lb. mushrooms, sliced
Season with: **1 T. soy sauce**
1/2 t. garlic powder
MSG (optional)

Heat through for not more than 5 minutes. *Do not overcook.* Serve immediately.

BROCCOLI RING—P

Serves eight.

In sauce pan, heat: **2 T. margarine**
Add and stir until smooth: **2 T. flour**
Gradually add and cook until thick: **1 cup milk substitute**
Add: **4 egg yolks, beaten**
2 packages frozen chopped broccoli, cooked and drained

Cool slightly.

Fold in: **4 egg whites, stiffly beaten**
salt and pepper
1 t. lemon juice
1/8 t. nutmeg

Pour into greased and floured 2-cup ring mold. Place in pan of boiling water and bake at 325° for 30 minutes.

CARROT SOUFFLÉ—P

Serves eight.

Combine in bowl: **1 cup sugar**
6 egg yolks
1 cup cooked carrots, mashed (about 1 lb.)
2 T. orange juice
1 T. lemon juice
1 cup grated blanched almonds

Fold in: **6 egg whites, stiffly beaten**

Pour into 2 1/2-quart soufflé dish. Bake at 350° for 45 minutes.

CARROT RINGS—P

Serves eight.

In sauce pan, cook until tender: **2 lbs. carrots**
salted water to cover

Drain and mash.

In small skillet, heat: **4 T. margarine**

Sauté: **1 small onion, chopped**

Stir onion into carrots.

Add: **1/4 cup chopped parsley**

1 1/2 t. salt
1/4 t. pepper

Pour into 8 greased 4-ounce ring molds. Chill until 30 minutes before serving time. Bake at 325° for 30 minutes. Unmold ring onto each serving plate. Spoon seasoned cooked peas into center of ring.

CAULIFLOWER IN MUSHROOM SAUCE—D

Serves six.

In sauce pan, cook according to directions and drain:	**2 pkgs. frozen cauliflower**
Add:	**1 can cream of mushroom soup**
	1/2 cup sour cream
	1/4 cup slivered toasted almonds

FRIED EGGPLANT—P

Serves four.

Peel and cut into 1/2" slices:	**1 medium eggplant**
Season with:	**salt, pepper, garlic powder**
Dip into:	**pre-seasoned bread crumbs**
In skillet, heat:	**2 T. oil**

Fry slices until browned lightly.

ORANGE-MINTED PEAS—P

Serves eight.

In small skillet, heat:	**1/2 cup margarine**
Add, heat, and steep for few minutes:	**3 T. slivered orange rind**

Add:	**1/4 cup mint, finely chopped**
When ready to serve, add orange-mint mixture to:	**3 pkgs. frozen peas, cooked according to directions and drained**

SPICED PEAS—P

Serves four.

Line heavy sauce pan with:	**3 or 4 large, wet, outside leaves of lettuce**
Place in lettuce:	**2 lbs. shelled peas**
Add:	**1 t. sugar**
	4 T. water
	1 stick cinnamon

Cover tightly and cook 20 minutes.

Add:	**1/2 t. ginger**

RATATOUILLE—P

Serves six.

In skillet, heat:	**1/3 cup oil**
Add and sauté until soft:	**1 large onion, sliced**
	2 cloves garlic, chopped
Add:	**2 zucchini, sliced**
	1 small eggplant, peeled and cubed
	2 green peppers, sliced
Sprinkle with:	**3 T. flour**

Mix gently. Cover and cook slowly, about 1 hour.

Add:	**5 tomatoes, sliced**
	salt

freshly ground pepper
1 T. capers

Simmer uncovered until mixture is thick. Serve hot or cold.

SHERRIED SPINACH—D or P

Serves four.

In small skillet, heat:	**1 T. margarine**
Sauté:	**1/4 lb. mushrooms, sliced**
Remove from heat and add to:	**1 pkg. frozen chopped spinach, cooked according to directions and drained**
	1 T. margarine
	dash nutmeg
	salt and pepper to taste
	2 T. dry sherry
When ready to serve, add:	**1/4 cup heavy cream** *or*
	1/4 cup milk substitute

Heat, sprinkle with croutons.

STRING BEANS, AMANDINE—P

Serves four.

In skillet, heat:	**3 T. margarine**
Add and sauté:	**1 cup almonds**
Pour over them:	**1 pkg. frozen French-cut string beans, cooked and drained**
Season with:	**salt**
	pinch of orégano

STRING BEANS WITH ANCHOVIES—P

Serves six to eight.

In small skillet, heat: **3 T. olive oil**

Add and heat: **1/4 cup capers**
1/4 cup anchovy filets
1 clove garlic, crushed

Remove from heat and add to: **2 pkgs. frozen Italian-style string beans, cooked and drained**
salt and pepper to taste

Sprinkle with: **onion, finely chopped**

SUMMER VEGETABLE PLATTER—M

Serves eight.

A beautiful blending of tones of green and yellow!

Marinade

In a sauce pan, combine and heat: **3 cups chicken stock**
1 cup dry white wine
1 cup olive oil
1/2 cup lemon juice
6 sprigs of parsley
2 large garlic cloves
1/2 t. thyme
10 peppercorns
1 t. salt

Cover and simmer for 45 minutes.
Strain marinade and return to pot.

To the marinade, add: **24 small peeled white onions**

Cover and cook for 20 minutes. Remove from heat with slotted spoon and place in large bowl and set aside.

Add to simmering marinade: **1 lb. zucchini, unpeeled and sliced**

1 lb. small yellow squash, unpeeled and sliced

Cook uncovered for 10 minutes. Add vegetables to bowl with onions, reserving marinade.

Add to simmering marinade: **3 medium green peppers, cut lengthwise into 1/2" strips**
1/2 lb. whole green beans

Cook for 8 minutes uncovered. Add to bowl. Taste and season the marinade. Pour over vegetables making sure that they are at least partially covered with hot marinade. Cover bowl tightly and place in refrigerator overnight. To serve, lift carefully with slotted spoon from marinade and arrange attractively on serving platter. Garnish with lemon slices.

TOMATOES, BROILED—P

Serves six.

Halve and arrange cut side up in shallow baking dish: **6 medium tomatoes**
Combine: **1/2 cup bread crumbs**
1/2 cup green olives, chopped
1 t. salt
1/2 t. basil
On each tomato half, place: **1 rounded T. of mixture**
Spoon on tomatoes: **3 T. olive oil**

Broil at high broiler heat about 3 inches from source, until tops are brown —about 10 minutes.

ZUCCHINI—P

Serves four to six.

In small sauce pan heat: **1 T. oil**
Sauté: **1 medium onion, thinly sliced**

Add: **3 medium zucchini, cut in half lengthwise**
1 t orégano
salt and pepper to taste
1 8-oz. can tomato sauce

Cover and cook until barely tender, 8–10 minutes.

Salads and Molds

ANTIPASTO—P

Serves eight or ten.

Marinate in large bowl:	**1 bottle Italian salad dressing**
	1 can anchovy filets
	1 can artichoke hearts
	1 can tuna fish
	1 can button mushrooms
	1/2 bottle capers
	1 bottle pearl onions
	1 stalk celery, diced

Serve on chunks of crisp lettuce.

Garnish with:	**1 jar black olives**
	1 jar green olives
	1 tin sardines
	2 hard-cooked eggs, quartered
	1/4 cup pimento, sliced
For M., add:	**thin slices of salami**
For D., add:	**thin slices of cheese**

BRANDIED FRUIT—P

Serves ten or twelve.

At least 10 days before serving, drain well and place in bowl to marinate: **1 large can peaches, quartered**
1 large can pears, quartered
1 large can apricots, halved
1 large can pineapple chunks
1 large can kadota figs
1 large jar maraschino cherries

Add: **1/2 pint brandy**
1/2 pint rum

Be sure to use only top quality canned fruits to give best appearance. Cover tightly. Refrigerate. When ready to serve, place in your prettiest glass bowl and serve in individual sherbet glasses or large-size, decorated paper dessert bowls.

CAESAR SALAD—P

Serves four to six.

In large salad bowl, place: **2 heads romaine, torn into pieces**
1 2-oz. can anchovies, drained

In large jar, combine: **1/3 cup salad oil**
1/2 t. salt
freshly ground black pepper
1 T. Worcestershire sauce
1/4 cup lemon juice
1/2 t. dry mustard

Cover jar and shake well. Pour over romaine in salad bowl.

Break over salad: **2 eggs, boiled for 60 seconds**

Sprinkle with: **1/2 cup croutons**

Note: For luncheon dish, add thin slices of salami and wedges of hard-cooked eggs, for **M**. For **D.**, add thin slices of cheese, chunks of tuna, and egg wedges.

COLE SLAW—P

Serves four to six.

In large mixing bowl, place: **1 head green cabbage, shredded**

Add: **2 t. onion, grated**
2 large carrots, grated
1 green pepper, diced

Combine and add to cabbage: **1/4 cup wine vinegar**
1/2 t. Tabasco sauce
salt
freshly ground black pepper
1 t. caraway seed
2 T. capers
1 1/2 cups mayonnaise
1 T. sugar

Toss and chill well.

CRANBERRY-ORANGE RELISH—P

Serves twelve.

In sauce pan, combine: **1 lb. cranberries, picked over and washed**
2 cups sugar
1/2 cup water
2 t. grated orange rind
1/2 cup orange juice

Cook until cranberries pop open—about 10 minutes. Skim foam from top.

Add: **1/2 cup blanched almonds, slivered**

Chill.

CUCUMBER SALAD—P

Serves four to six.

Peel and slice thin: **2 medium cucumbers**
1 onion
Marinate in: **1/2 bottle Italian salad dressing**

Serve in individual dishes.

HOT FRUIT COMPOTE—P

Serves 12

Crumb Mixture

Mix together: **1/2 cup brown sugar**
1/2 cup slivered almonds
grated rind of 3 oranges and 3 lemons

In a large baking dish, arrange in layers: **3 small cans apricot halves, drained**
2 #2 cans pineapple chunks, drained
1 #2 1/2 can sliced peaches, drained
3 oranges, peeled and sliced thin
3 lemons, peeled and sliced thin
2 #2 1/2 cans pitted black Bing cherries for top layer

Sprinkle crumb mixture over each layer. Heat at 400° for 15 minutes. This may be served as a meat accompaniment or as a dessert laced with Cointreau.

GREEN BEAN SALAD—P

Serves six.

In bowl, marinate for 30 minutes:	**1 lb. cold cooked green beans**
Covered with:	**French dressing**
Mix beans with:	**1 cup celery, diced**
Garnish salad with:	**chopped chives**
	hard-cooked egg white, grated
	hard-cooked egg yolk, grated

Chill.

GREEN BEAN SALAD #2—M

Serves six.

Cook 10 minutes and immediately pour cold water over, to prevent further cooking:	**1 lb. green beans**

Marinate them 1 hour.

Marinade

In small bowl, combine:	**3 T. wine vinegar**
	3 T. olive oil
	1/2 cup chicken broth
	1 t. salt
	freshly ground pepper
	1 t. finely chopped fresh dill
	1 t. finely chopped parsley

Blend well with wire whisk.
Serve well chilled. You may garnish the bowl with rings of red onion.

MIXED GREEN SALAD—P

Serves ten.

In large salad bowl, break up:	**2 heads romaine**
	1 head Boston lettuce
	1 head Chinese cabbage
Add:	**1 small bunch scallions, chopped**
	1 green pepper, sliced
	1 red onion, sliced
	1 can hearts of palm, chopped
	1 jar artichoke hearts, drained

Arrange unpeeled cucumber spears around outside edge of salad bowl. Toss lightly with garlic dressing.

APRICOT MOLD—D

Serves twelve.

Drain:	**1 large can apricot halves**
Add to the syrup:	**water to make 2 cups**
Heat syrup and dissolve in it:	**2 pkgs. apricot jello**

Cool.

Add:	**2 cups sour cream**

Beat with rotary beater.

Add:	**1/2 jar baby-food apricot-apples**
	1 jar baby-food apricot-tapioca

Beat again.

Fold in:	**the apricot halves**

Pour into oiled 2-quart ring mold. Chill until firm. Unmold and garnish with fresh apricots and cherries, in season, or orange slices and green grapes.

BURGUNDY MOLD—P

Serves ten to twelve.

Drain: **1 large can Bing cherries**
In bowl, dissolve: **2 pkgs. black cherry jello**
In heated: **1 1/2 cups Burgundy wine**
1/2 cup cherry syrup

Cool.

Remove pits and fold in: **the cherries**

Pour into oiled 2-quart ring mold. Chill until firm. Unmold and garnish with purple grapes.

CRANBERRY-CELERY MOLD—P

Serves twelve.

Drain: **1 medium can crushed pineapple**
Add to the syrup: **water to make 3 cups**

Heat.

In bowl, dissolve in the hot syrup: **2 pkgs. red jello**

Place in refrigerator until partially set (consistency of egg whites.)

Fold in: **1 cup diced celery**
1 cup chopped walnuts
1 can cranberry jelly, mashed smooth
the drained pineapple

Pour into oiled 2-quart ring mold. Chill until firm. Unmold and serve.

GINGER ALE MOLD—P

Serves sixteen.

Drain: **1 large can sliced peaches**
In bowl, dissolve: **2 pkgs. lemon jello**
In: **1 cup peach syrup, heated**
Add: **1 cup ginger ale**

Pour into oiled 3-quart ring mold. Chill until partially set.

Arrange in mold: **the drained peaches**
maraschino cherries

Chill until set.

Drain: **1 large can pineapple chunks**
Add to the syrup: **water to make 1 1/2 cups.**
Heat syrup and dissolve in it: **1 pkg. lime jello**

Refrigerate until partially set.

Fold in: **the pineapple chunks**

Pour into mold over first layer. Chill until set.

Drain: **1 large can fruits for salad**
Add to the syrup: **water to make 3 cups**
Heat syrup and dissolve in it: **2 pkgs. raspberry jello**

Chill until partially set.

Fold in: **the fruits for salad**

Pour into mold over second layer and chill until set.

LIME MOLD—D

Serves sixteen.

In bowl, dissolve: **2 pkgs. lime jello**
In: **3 cups hot water**

Pour into oiled 3-quart ring mold. Chill until partially set.

Arrange in jello: **maraschino cherries**

Chill until set.

Drain: **1 medium can crushed pineapple**
Add to the syrup: **water to make 3 3/4 cups**
Heat syrup and dissolve in it: **2 pkgs. lime jello**

Cool.

Fold in: **1 pt. sour cream**
the crushed pineapple

Pour into mold and chill until set. When ready to serve, place bowl of melted strawberry ice cream in center of ring.

ORANGE MOLD—P

Serves twelve.

Drain, separating syrups: **1 can mandarin oranges**
1 can crushed pineapple
Add to the pineapple syrup: **water to make 3 cups**
Heat syrup and dissolve in it: **3 pkgs. orange jello**

Place in refrigerator until partially set.

With electric mixer, beat in: **1 pt. orange water ice, softened**
Fold in: **the oranges and pineapple**

Pour into oiled 2-quart ring mold. Chill until set. Unmold and garnish with kumquats.

RED WHITE AND BLUE MOLD—D

Serves sixteen.

Drain: **1 medium can peach halves**
1 medium can crushed pineapple
1 can blueberries

Line bottom of oiled 3-quart mold with: **the peach halves, placed cut side down with maraschino cherry under center of each**

In bowl, dissolve: **1 pkg. raspberry jello**

In: **3/4 cup boiling water**
3/4 cup peach syrup

Chill until partially set. Pour gently over peaches. Chill until set.

In bowl, dissolve: **2 pkgs. lemon jello**

In: **1 1/2 cups boiling water**
1 1/2 cups pineapple juice

Chill until partially set.

Fold in mixture of: **1 cup crushed pineapple**
1 cup sour cream blended smooth with
1 8-oz. pkg. cream cheese

Pour over first layer.

In bowl, dissolve: **1 pkg. black raspberry jello**

In: **3/4 cup boiling water**
3/4 cup blueberry juice

Chill until partially set.

Fold in: **1 can blueberries**

Pour over second layer. Chill until set. Unmold and serve with Lemon Mayonnaise.

STRAWBERRY-CHEESE MOLD—D

Serves ten.

In oiled 10-inch ring mold evenly space: **12 cheese balls**

Cheese Balls

Shape into 12 balls:	**2 3-oz. pkgs. cream cheese, softened with cream**
Roll in:	**1/2 cup nuts, finely chopped**
In mold, cover cheese balls with:	**layer of strawberries, lightly sugared**
In bowl, dissolve:	**1 pkg. strawberry jello**
In:	**2 cups hot water**

Cool and pour over cheese balls and strawberries. Chill until set. Unmold and garnish with large strawberries. Place bowl of melted pineapple sherbet in center of ring.

STRAWBERRY-RHUBARB MOLD—P

Serves six to eight.

In bowl, dissolve:	**2 pkgs. strawberry jello**
In:	**1 cup boiling water**
Combine and add to jello:	**syrup from 1 pkg. frozen strawberries, defrosted and drained**
	syrup from 1 pkg. frozen cooked rhubarb
	syrup from 1 medium can crushed pineapple, drained
	enough water to syrups to total 3 cups liquid

Chill until partially set.

Add:	**drained fruits**

Chill until firm. Unmold and garnish with fresh strawberries.

POTATO SALAD—M

Serves four to six.

In sauce pan, boil until tender but still firm—about 30 minutes: **8 medium potatoes**

Peel potatoes while still warm and cut into slices 1/2 inches thick. Place in salad bowl.

In another bowl, combine and mix well:

1 T. salt
1/2 t. freshly ground black pepper
1/4 cup wine vinegar
2 T. clear chicken broth
2 T. white wine
1/2 T. tarragon
1 T. chopped parsley
1/2 cup oil

Pour over potatoes and toss gently until all liquid is absorbed. May be served warm or cold.

SALAD VARIATIONS—P

#1. In large salad bowl rubbed with garlic clove, place:

chunks of iceberg lettuce
small whole tomatoes
1″ chunks of cucumber
1″ chunks of carrots
1″ pieces of celery
1″ slices of green pepper
whole white part of scallions
whole radishes
1/2 cup chick peas

Toss with desired dressing.

#2. On large oblong platter, arrange in rows:

thin-sliced tomatoes
thin-sliced cucumber

thin-sliced red onion
radish roses
carrot sticks
whole scallions
stalks of celery hearts

Serve with desired dressing.

#3. For a smörgåsbord effect, add to variation #2 rows of:

anchovies
sardines
pickled herring
hard-cooked eggs, sliced

TOMATO-ARTICHOKE SALAD—P

Serves eight or ten.

Combine in glass salad bowl:

2 pints cherry tomatoes or
2 lbs. tomatoes, cut in wedges
3 6-oz. jars marinated artichokes, drained
1 t. basil
1 t. orégano

Toss with Italian dressing.

WALDORF SALAD—P

Serves six.

In bowl, combine:

6 medium apples, red skin on, diced
2 cups celery, diced
1/2 cup broken walnuts

Toss with mayonnaise. Serve on lettuce cups.

WATERFORD SALAD

Serves six.

Arrange in shallow glass bowl or individual glass serving dishes, layers of:

- **1 pkg. frozen chopped spinach, cooked**
- **1 large can jullienne strips of beets**
- **2 hard-cooked eggs, separated and grated.**

Serve with Italian dressing.

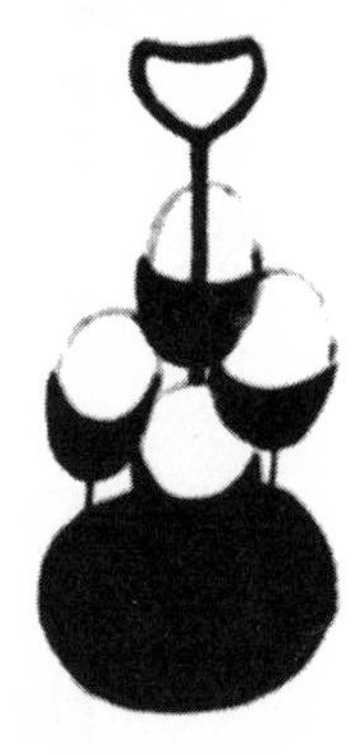

EGGS FOO YONG—P

Serves six.

In bowl, combine: **6 eggs, well beaten**
1 can bean sprouts, drained
2 T. minced onion
1 t. salt
1/2 t. pepper
1 cup tuna fish

Fry in vegetable oil in skillet as you would pancakes, turning once to cook other side. Serve with sauce.

Sauce

In sauce pan, cook until thick, stirring constantly: **1 T. cornstarch**
3 T. soy sauce
1 T. sugar
1 1/2 cups water

Batter may be prepared in advance and pancakes made at last minute.

SCRAMBLED EGGS

Each variation serves four people.

#1. With Smoked Salmon-D

In skillet, heat:	**3 T. butter**
Add and sauté:	**1 onion, chopped**
	1 green pepper, chopped
Add and heat through:	**1/2 lb. smoked salmon, cut in pieces**
	2 tomatoes, chopped
	freshly ground black pepper
Beat with fork and add:	**6 eggs and**
	6 T. milk

When mixture begins to set at bottom and sides, lift cooked portions with spatula. Turn gently so as to cook all portions evenly. Place in 400° oven for 3–5 minutes to puff up and brown. Serve immediately.

#2. With Mushrooms-D

In skillet, heat:	**1/4 cup butter**
Add and sauté 5 minutes:	**1/2 lb. mushrooms, chopped**
Add:	**2 t. minced chives**
Beat with fork and add:	**6 eggs**
	6 T. cream
	salt
	freshly ground black pepper

Follow method of cooking as above.

#3. Herbed-D

In skillet, heat to sizzling:	**3 T. butter**
Beat with fork and add:	**6 eggs**
	1/2 pint sour cream
	1/2 t. dry mustard
	1 t. tarragon
	1 t. chopped parsley

salt
freshly ground black pepper

Follow method for cooking as above.

LOX-SALMON SOUFFLÉ—D

Serves twelve.

In a skillet, heat:	**2 T. butter**
Sauté:	**2 onions**
In a bowl, beat:	**12 eggs**
Add:	**2 cups milk**
	1-lb. can red salmon, drained
	1/4 lb. salted lox
	1/4 lb. unsalted lox
	dash of pepper
Fold in:	**sautéed onions**

Pour mixture into greased 9 × 13″ baking dish. Bake at 350°, 45 minutes or until puffy and browned.

MUSHROOM SOUFFLÉ—D

Serves eight or ten.

Make the filling for the soufflé first, so that it's warm and ready to spread when soufflé is ready.

Filling

In large skillet, heat:	**4 T. olive oil**
Sauté until golden:	**2 large onions, chopped**
Add:	**3/4 lb. finely chopped mushrooms**

Cook over low heat until tender. Remove from heat.

Add: **4 T. sour cream**
4 T. chopped scallions
2 T. lemon juice
salt and pepper

Mix through and set aside.

Soufflé Roll

In a sauce pan, melt: **4 T. butter**
Blend in: **1/2 cup flour**
1/2 t. salt
1/8 t. white pepper
Gradually stir in: **2 cups milk**

Bring to the boil, stirring constantly. Cook one minute.

In small bowl, mix: **5 egg yolks**

Add a little hot mixture to egg yolks and return it all to sauce pan. Cook over medium heat for one minute, stirring constantly. Do not allow mixture to boil. Set aside and cool to room temperature, stirring occasionally.

In a bowl, beat until stiff, not dry: **5 egg whites**

Fold into cooled egg-yolk mixture.
Pour into 15 1/2 × 10 1/2" jelly-roll pan which has been greased, lined with waxed paper, and greased again (important). Bake at 400°, 25–30 minutes until puffed and brown.
Turn soufflé roll immediately onto a kitchen towel. Remove waxed paper and spread with warm filling. Roll up as you would a jelly roll using the towel as an aid. Slide onto an oblong serving platter, seam side down. Garnish with parsley. Slice and serve accompanied with a bowl of sour cream. The soufflé freezes very well but must be removed from the freezer early in the day, because it takes a long while to defrost. Let it defrost on wire cooling rack. Reheat at 375° until heated through.

OMELETS

Each omelet serves two.

In small bowl, combine: **3 eggs**
3 T. cold water
salt
pepper

Beat thoroughly with fork until light and foamy.

In 10 inch skillet, heat to sizzling: **3 T. margarine**

Pour eggs into pan. Shake pan back and forth. Cook slowly, keeping heat low. As bottom begins to set, lift up slightly with spatula to let uncooked portion flow underneath and cook. Place filling on half of omelet. When eggs seem set, fold or roll omelet over filling. Place omelet on heated serving dish or in chafing dish. Garnish with remaining sauce.

FILLINGS

Enough for three omelets.

#1. *Chasseur*-M

In skillet, melt: **3 T. margarine**

Add: **2 t. chopped shallots or scallions**
3 chicken livers, broiled and cut into 3 or 4 pieces
3 mushrooms, sliced
salt
freshly ground black pepper

Cook gently, stirring for one minute.

Sprinkle mixture with: **1 1/2 t. flour**
3 T. white wine

Garnish with: **18 small mushroom caps, sautéed in 3 T. margarine**
parsley, chopped

#2. *Spanish*-P

In skillet, heat:	**3 T. oil**
Add and sauté 5 minutes:	**1 onion, chopped**
	1 green pepper, chopped
	1 stalk celery, chopped
	1 leek, chopped
	1/2 t. fennel seed
	1 clove garlic, minced
	3 t. chopped parsley
Add:	**6 tomatoes, chopped**
	1 clove
	1/2 t. thyme
	1/2 t. orégano
	1/2 bay leaf
	salt
	freshly ground black pepper

Simmer gently until vegetables are tender, 10 minutes. Remove clove and bay leaf.

See Index for additional egg recipes.

Breads

APRICOT-NUT BREAD—P

Serves ten to twelve.

In bowl, mix together:	**3/4 cup white sugar**
	1/2 cup brown sugar
	1 T. soft shortening
	1 egg
Pre-soak:	**1 1/2 cups cut-up dried apricots**
In:	**1 1/2 cups boiling water**

Cool, and add apricots and water to sugar mixture.

Stir in:	**2 1/4 cups all-purpose flour**
	1 t. baking soda
	1/2 t. salt
	1 cup broken nuts

Pour into well-greased 9 × 5 × 3″ loaf pan. Let stand 20 minutes before baking. Bake at 350° 50 to 60 minutes until it tests done. Serve warm or cold.

DATE NUT BREAD—P

Serves ten to twelve.

In bowl, combine and mix well: **1 lb. dates, cut up**
2 cups boiling water
1/4 cup margarine
4 t. baking soda
1 t. salt

In another bowl, beat: **2 eggs**
2 cups sugar

Add to date mixture.

Stir in: **3 cups all-purpose flour**
2 t. vanilla
juice and grated rind of 1 orange

Fold in: **1/2 cups nuts, chopped**

Pour batter into 2 well-greased 9 × 5 × 3″ loaf pans. Let stand 20 minutes before baking to reduce the size of the crack on the top of the loaf. Bake at 350° for 1–1 1/4 hours, until it tests done.

ORANGE HONEY BREAD—P

Serves ten to twelve.

In mixing bowl, combine and mix well: **2 T. soft shortening**
1 cup honey

Add: **1 egg**
1 1/2 T. grated orange rind

Add alternately: **2 1/2 cups all-purpose flour**
2 1/2 t. baking powder
1/2 t. soda
1/2 t. salt
3/4 cup orange juice

Stir just until flour is moistened and ingredients are blended.

Add: **3/4 cup nuts, chopped**

Pour into well-greased 9 × 5 × 3″ loaf pan. Before putting it into oven, let stand for 20 minutes. This reduces the size of the crack usually found in loaf breads. Bake at 325°, 1 hour and 10 minutes.

SWEET-DOUGH YEAST BREADS—D

In large bowl, mix together:	**1 cup lukewarm milk**
	1/2 cup sugar
	1 t. salt
Crumble into mixture and stir until dissolved:	**2 cakes compressed yeast**
Stir in:	**2 eggs**
	1/4 cup soft shortening
	1/4 cup soft butter
Mix in, first with spoon then with hand:	**4 1/2–5 cups all-purpose flour**

When dough begins to leave sides of bowl, turn it out onto lightly floured board to knead. Use minimum amount of flour to keep dough as soft as possible, *almost sticky, just able to be handled.* Knead dough until smooth, elastic, and doesn't stick to board. Place in greased bowl, turning once to bring greased side up. Cover with damp cloth and let rise in warm, draft-free spot, (about 80°) until doubled, 1 1/2–2 hours. Punch dough down and turn it completely over in bowl. Let rise again until almost doubled in bulk, 30–45 minutes.

VARIATIONS

#1. *Pecan Rolls* 1 1/2 dozen.
Divide dough into 3 sections. Cover and let rest 15 minutes, so that dough is easy to handle. Roll each section into 9 × 18″ oblong.

Spread surface with:	**2 T. soft butter**
Sprinkle with:	**1/2 cup sugar**
	2 t. cinnamon
	raisins

Roll up like jelly roll beginning at wide side. Cut roll into 1-inch slices. Place cut slices in muffin cups coated with: **1/2 cup melted butter**
1/2 cup brown sugar
1/2 cup pecan halves

Cover and let rise until double in bulk, 35–40 minutes. Bake at 375°, 25–30 minutes until golden brown. Turn upside down and let pan stay over rolls 1 minute, so that syrup runs down over rolls. May be frozen. When ready to serve, reheat wrapped in tin foil.

#2. *Swedish Tea Ring*-D
Follow recipe above for Pecan Rolls up to point where dough is rolled as for jelly roll.
Place sealed edge down in ring form on lightly greased baking sheet. Seal by pinching edges of the roll together. With scissors moistened in warm water, cut 2/3 of way through ring at 1-inch intervals. Turn each section on its side. Let rise and bake as for Pecan Rolls. Frost while warm with Confectioner's Sugar Icing, and decorate with nuts and maraschino cherries.

APPLE MUFFINS—P

Serves twelve.

In mixing bowl, combine: **1 1/2 cups all-purpose flour**
1/2 cup sugar
2 t. baking powder
1/2 t. salt
1/2 t. cinnamon

Add: **1/4 cup soft shortening**
1 cup unpared, grated raw apple
1 egg
1/2 cup milk substitute

Stir just until flour is moistened and ingredients are blended. Batter will look lumpy. Fill well-greased muffin cups 2/3 full.

Sprinkle tops with mixture of:
1/3 cup brown sugar
1/3 cup broken nuts
1/2 t. cinnamon

Bake at 400° 25–30 minutes. When ready to serve, wrap in tin foil and reheat thoroughly at 400°, 15 minutes.

BLUEBERRY MUFFINS—P

Serves twelve.

In mixing bowl, combine:
1 1/2 cups all-purpose flour
1/2 cup sugar
2 t. baking powder
1/2 t. salt

Add and blend together:
1/4 cup soft shortening
1 egg
1/2 cup apricot nectar

Fold in:
3/4 cup canned blueberries
or
1 cup fresh blueberries

Fill well-greased or paper-lined muffin cups 2/3 full. Sprinkle tops with sugar. Bake at 400°, 20–25 minutes. When ready to serve, wrap in tin foil and reheat at 400° for 15 minutes.

ORANGE HONEY MUFFINS—P

Serves twelve.

In mixing bowl, combine:
1 1/2 cups all-purpose flour
1/2 cup sugar
2 t. baking powder
1/2 t. salt

Add and blend together:
1/4 cup soft shortening
2 eggs

1/4 cup orange juice
1/4 cup honey

In bottom of each well-greased muffin cup, place: **1 t. honey**
1 thin slice unpeeled orange, quartered

Spoon batter on top, filling cups 2/3 full. Bake at 400°, 20–25 minutes. Serve orange slice up.

BELMONT SWEET ROLLS—P

3 1/2 dozen.

In large bowl, mix: **2 cups flour**
1/2 cup sugar
1 1/2 t. salt
2 pkgs. dry yeast
1/4 lb. margarine (soft)

Gradually add: **1 1/2 cups hot water**

Beat 2 minutes.

Add: **2 eggs**
1/2 cup flour

Beat 2 more minutes. The batter will be thick and wet.
Remove dough onto floured board and knead in 3–3 1/2 cups of flour. Put back into bowl. Cover bowl with plastic wrap and kitchen towel. Let stand at room temperature for 20 minutes. Place bowl in refrigerator for 2 hours. It will rise double in bulk.
To shape rolls, roll a section of dough on floured board into 9 × 18" oblong. Spread surface with 2 tablespoons soft margarine.

Sprinkle with: **1/2 cup brown sugar**
1/2 t. maple extract
raisins and chopped nuts

Roll up like jelly roll beginning at wide side. Cut roll into 1-inch slices and place into muffin cups which have been coated with 1/2 cup melted margarine, 1/2 cup brown sugar, 1/2 cup pecan halves. Cover and let rise for 1 hour. Bake at 350° (not preheated) about 30 minutes until golden brown. Turn upside down and let pan stay over rolls 1 minute, so that syrup runs down over rolls. May be frozen. When ready to serve, reheat.

CINNAMON TWISTS—D

Eighteen twists.

In large sauce pan, heat to lukewarm:	**1 cup sour crean**
Remove from heat and stir in:	**3 T. sugar**
	1/8 t. baking soda
	1 t. salt
Crumble into mixture and stir until dissolved:	**1 cake compressed yeast**
Add and mix well:	**1 large egg**
	2 T. soft shortening
	3 cups all-purpose flour

Turn dough onto floured board and fold over several times until smooth. Roll into an oblong 24 × 6 inches.

Spread dough with:	**2 T. soft butter**
Sprinkle half with:	**1/3 cup brown sugar**
	1 t. cinnamon

Fold other half over. Cut into 24 1-inch strips. Hold each strip at both ends and twist in opposite directions. Place on greased baking sheet 2 inches apart. Press both ends of twists onto baking sheet. Cover and let rise for 1 hour. Bake at 375° 15 minutes and frost with Confectioner's Sugar Icing.

Sauces and Dressings

BARBECUE SAUCE—P

2 1/2–3 cups.

Combine in bowl:

1 cup vinegar
2/3 cup salad oil
2 t. Worcestershire sauce
2 drops Tabasco
2 T. grated onion
1 clove garlic, minced
1 1/2 t. salt
1/2 t. paprika
1 can tomato paste
1/2 t. dry mustard

Use as marinade for Short Ribs, London Broil or chicken, or pour over Meat Loaf before baking.

BÉARNAISE SAUCE—P

3/4–1 cup.

In skillet, combine:
2 T. white wine
1 T. tarragon vinegar
2 t. chopped tarragon
2 t. chopped shallots
1/4 t. freshly ground black pepper

Bring to boil and cook rapidly until almost all liquid disappears.

In small sauce pan, heat: **1/2 cup margarine**

In blender, place:
3 egg yolks
2 T. lemon juice
1/4 t. salt
pinch cayenne pepper

Cover and flick motor on and off at high speed. Remove cover, turn motor on high and gradually add the hot (but not browned) margarine. Add herb mixture. Cover and blend on high speed 4 seconds. Serve hot immediately with steak or roast beef.

RED CAVIAR SALAD DRESSING—P

2 cups.

In bowl, combine:
1 1/2 cups mayonnaise
1/4 cup ketchup
1/4 cup vinegar
2 T. red caviar
1/2 t. garlic powder
dash of salt

Refrigerate in tightly covered container. Serve with hearts of lettuce.

CHERRY-ORANGE SAUCE—P

1–1 1/2 cups.

In sauce pan, combine:
4 t. cornstarch
4 T. sugar
1/4 t. salt
1/4 t. dry mustard
1/4 t. ginger

Add:
liquid from 1-lb. can sour, red, pitted, water-packed cherries
1 T. slivered orange rind
1/2 cup orange juice
1/4 cup currant jelly
few drops red food coloring

Place over medium heat and cook, stirring constantly, until mixture boils and thickens.

Add:
drained cherries
2 T. sherry

When ready to serve, reheat. Serve with roast turkey or chicken.

CUMBERLAND SAUCE—P

1 1/2 cups.

In sauce pan, combine and simmer until smooth:
1 cup red currant jelly
1 6-oz. can frozen orange juice concentrate
4 T. sherry
1 t. dry mustard
1/8 t. ginger
1/4 t. Tabasco

Serve with cold chicken or beef.

FROZEN HORSERADISH SQUARES—D

Twelve squares.

In bowl, combine:
1/2 cup freshly shredded horseradish
1 cup heavy cream, whipped
2 t. sugar
salt
freshly ground black pepper
1 t. chopped dill

Place in icecube trays and freeze. When ready to serve, remove from trays. Serve with fish.

LEMON MAYONNAISE—D

1 1/2 cups.

In mixing bowl, combine:
1/2 cup mayonnaise
1/4 cup frozen lemonade concentrate, defrosted

Fold in:
1/2 cup heavy cream, whipped

Refrigerate in tightly covered container. Serve with fish or fruit salad.

LEMON SAUCE—M

1 1/2 cups.

In a sauce pan, place:
3/4 cup sugar
1/2 cup white vinegar
1 cup chicken broth
1 T. corn starch mixed with
2 T. water
1 t. MSG (optional)
1 lemon—juice and finely-chopped thin yellow rind

Bring to boil, stirring until mixture thickens.

Add:	**3 small carrots, cut in strips**
	1/2 large green pepper, cut in strips
	3 scallions, cut in strips
	1/2 cup crushed pineapple
Remove from heat and stir in:	**1 1-oz. bottle of lemon extract**

Serve over Chinese Fried Chicken.

MUSHROOM GRAVY—M

Serves six.

In skillet, heat:	**1 T. margarine**
Add and sauté 5 minutes:	**3/4 lb. mushrooms, thinly sliced**

Set aside.

In sauce pan, heat:	**1 T. margarine**
Add:	**1 T. chopped parsley**
	1/2 clove garlic, chopped fine
	1 small onion, chopped

Cook over medium heat 3 minutes.

Stir in:	**1 T. flour**
Gradually add:	**1 cup clear beef broth**

Stir constantly.

Add:	**sautéed mushrooms**

Simmer 15 minutes. Serve hot with turkey, chicken or brisket.

CURRIED ONION SAUCE—M

4 cups.

In skillet, sauté until tender but not brown:	**1 large green apple, peeled, cored, finely chopped** **2 stalks celery, finely diced** **1/4 cup margarine**
Add and sauté 8–10 minutes longer:	**8 medium yellow onions, cut into 1/4″ slices**
Sprinkle with:	**3 T. flour** **4 t. curry powder** **1/4 t. salt**

Cook 3 minutes stirring continuously.

Stir in and bring to boil:	**3 cups clear chicken broth**
Add:	**1/4 cup seedless raisins (optional)**

Cook about 10 minutes, until onions are almost tender but still retain their form. Serve hot with broiled or grilled meats.

SAUTÉED ONION RINGS—P

Serves eight.

In skillet, heat:	**3 T. margarine**
Add and sauté:	**2 medium yellow onions, cut into 1/8″ slices, separated into rings**
Stir in:	**2 4-oz. cans sliced mushrooms** **salt to taste** **freshly ground black pepper**

Serve hot spooned over roast beef.

PIQUANT SAUCE—P

1 cup.

Prepare as for Velvet Sauce, except use one cup hot tomato juice in place of chicken or fish stock.

Add:
1 t. grated onion
3 T. finely chopped sour pickle
1 t. minced parsley

Serve over beef, chicken or fish.

REMOULADE—P

1 cup.

In bowl, combine:
3 T. wine vinegar
1 t. dry mustard
2 T. minced scallions
2 T. minced celery
1 t. fresh horseradish
1 T. minced parsley
1/2 cup and 1 T. olive oil
salt to taste
freshly ground black pepper
dash red pepper

Refrigerate. Serve with cold flaked fish.

SALMON SAUCE—P

1 cup.

In double boiler, combine and heat:
1/4 cup margarine
1 t. dry mustard
juice of 1 lemon
1/4 t. nutmeg

2 t. chopped parsley
1 t. chopped chives
salt
freshly ground black pepper

Stir with wire whisk until margarine has melted.

Add while beating: **4 egg yolks, beaten until thick and lemon colored**

Continue beating until sauce thickens. Serve hot with salmon.

VELVET SAUCE—M or P

1 cup.

In skillet, heat: **2 T. margarine**
Add: **2 T. flour**

Stir with wire whisk on and off the heat for 5 minutes. *Do not brown.*

Add while stirring constantly: **1 cup hot chicken (M) or fish (P) stock**

Bring to boil. Simmer 5 minutes.

Season with: **salt to taste**
freshly ground black pepper
pinch nutmeg
Stir in: **1/2 cup green seedless grapes, if desired**

Serve hot immediately over fish or chicken crêpes or use as basic white sauce. [Do not attempt to make white sauce with a dairy substitute. It curdles, and turns the sauce brown.]

VINAIGRETTE—P

1 cup.

In bowl, combine:
3/4 cup olive oil
1/4 cup lemon juice
salt to taste
1/2 t. dry mustard
freshly ground black pepper
1 T. chopped capers
1 t. finely chopped pickles
1/2 t. chopped parsley
1/2 t. chopped chervil
1/2 t. chopped chives

Mix well and chill. Serve over asparagus, broccoli, or cold flaked fish.

ZABAGLIONE—P

Serves six.

In mixing bowl, beat until thick and lemon colored: **6 egg yolks**
Add gradually while beating: **6 T. sugar**
2/3 cup sweet white wine

Place mixture over hot water and whip thoroughly with wire whisk until mixture foams up in pan and begins to thicken. *Do not overcook.* Serve warm over sherbet or water ice, or in dessert dishes.

Cakes

ANGEL-WATERMELON CAKE—P

Serves sixteen.

In large mixing bowl, prepare egg-white packet from:	**1 pkg. angel food cake mix**
Follow directions on box and add to required water: 1 bottle red food coloring	
Add as directed:	**flour packet**

Set bowl aside.

In second mixing bowl, prepare egg-white packet from:	**1 pkg. angel food cake mix**
Follow directions on box and add, to make water medium yellow-green:	**green and yellow food coloring**
Add:	**flour packet as directed**

Spread green batter on bottom and sides of 2 deep 4-quart metal bowls. Spread 1 cup red batter on bottom of each bowl. Sprinkle on about 10

chocolate bits. Add more batter, sprinkle more chocolate bits. Repeat until all batter is used, ending with batter. Bake at 375° 30–40 minutes, until top is well browned.
Remove from oven and immediately slice off any cake that may have risen above top of bowls. Turn bowls over and cool on wire rack. When cakes are completely cooled, remove from bowls and frost all but flat surface with Creamy Frosting tinted to deep green rind color. Cut one cake into 8 "watermelon" wedges. Keep other cake upright. May be propped with cake scraps.

APPLE CAKE—P

Serves twelve or fourteen.

In 1 quart measuring cup, combine:
3 cups apples, peeled, cored, and diced
5 T. sugar
5 t. cinnamon

In large mixing bowl, place:
3 cups flour
2 cups sugar
3 t. baking powder
1 t. salt

Make a well and add:
1 cup oil
4 eggs
1/4 cup orange juice
1 t. vanilla

Mix well with large spoon.
Grease and flour a 10-inch tube pan. Spoon about one-half the batter into pan. Spread apple mixture over batter. Spoon remaining batter over apples. Bake at 325° on middle rack of oven for 1 hour and 15 minutes until done.

APPLESAUCE CAKE—P

Serves twelve.

In mixing bowl, combine:	**2 1/2 cups all-purpose flour**
	2 cups sugar
	1/4 t. baking powder
	1 1/2 t. baking soda
	1 1/2 t. salt
	3/4 t. cinnamon
	1/2 t. cloves
	1/2 t. allspice
Add and beat 2 minutes:	**1/2 cup soft shortening**
	1/2 cup water
	1/2 cup walnuts, cut up
	1 cup raisins
Add and beat 2 minutes:	**1 1/2 cups apple sauce**
	1 large egg

Bake in greased and floured 9 × 13″ oblong pan, 350°, 45–50 minutes. When cool, place paper doily over cake.

Sprinkle with:	**confectioner's sugar**

Lift doily.

APPLESAUCE CAKE #2—P

Serves twelve or fourteen.

In mixing bowl, cream:	**1/2 cup margarine**
	1 cup sugar
Add and beat well:	**2 eggs**
Combine:	**2 1/2 cups flour**
	1/4 t. baking soda
	1 t. salt
	1/4 t. cinnamon
	1/4 t. nutmeg
	1/4 t. allspice

Add to mixing bowl alternately

with combination of: **1 cup applesauce**
1/4 cup orange juice

Fold in: **3/4 cup mixed dried fruits**
1/2 cup dark raisins
1 T. orange rind, grated
1 cup nuts, chopped fine

Grease well and flour a 10 inch tube pan. Pour batter into prepared pan. Bake at 325° for 1 1/2 hours, until it tests done. Let cake cool for 15 minutes and remove from pan.

Drizzle over warm cake: **1/2 cup rum**

BUNDT CAKE—D

Serves twelve to fourteen.

In mixing bowl, cream: **1 cup butter**
1 cup granulated sugar
1 cup powdered sugar

Add: **4 egg yolks, one at a time**
1 t. vanilla
1 t. almond

Add alternately a combination of: **3 cups flour**
2 t. baking powder
pinch of salt
and
1 cup milk

Fold in: **4 egg whites, stiffly beaten**

Grease a Bundt pan. Put dabs of butter in creases of mold and a drop of almond extract on each dab. Pour batter into pan. Bake at 350° for 1 1/2 hours. Let stand for 15 minutes before turning cake out of pan.

CARAMEL CAKE—P

Eight to ten servings.

First caramelize enough sugar for cake and frosting.

In heavy skillet over low heat, melt:	**3/4 cup sugar**

Stir constantly until sugar becomes a golden brown syrup.

Stir in:	**3/4 cup boiling water**

Stir over low heat, until lumps are dissolved.

Pour into measuring cup and add:	**enough cold water to make 1 1/3 cups liquid**
In mixing bowl, combine:	**2 1/8 cups all-purpose flour**
	1 cup sugar
	3 t. baking powder
	1 t. salt
Add and beat 2 minutes:	**1/2 cup soft shortening**
	3/4 cup caramel mixture
Add and beat 2 minutes:	**2 eggs**
	1/4 cup caramel mixture

Bake in greased and floured 9 × 13″ oblong pan 35–40 minutes or two 9″ layer pans at 350° 25–30 minutes. Frost with Caramel Icing.

CHIFFON CAKE—P

Serves twelve to fourteen.

Cherry-Nut

In small mixing bowl, combine:	**2 cups all-purpose flour**
	1 1/2 cups sugar
	3 t. baking powder
	1 t. salt
Make a "well" and add:	**1/2 cup salad oil**
	7 egg yolks, unbeaten

	1/2 cup cold water
	1 t. vanilla
	1/4 cup maraschino cherry juice
Beat with spoon until smooth.	
In large mixing bowl, beat until stiff peaks form:	**7 egg whites**
	1/2 t. cream of tartar
Fold in gently until just blended:	**Egg yolk mixture**
Fold in with few strokes:	**1/2 cup nuts, finely chopped**
	1/2 cup maraschino cherries, well drained and chopped

Bake in ungreased 10-inch tube pan, 325° for 55 minutes, then at 350° 10–15 minutes. When cake tests done, invert over soda bottle until cold.

Frost with Snowy White Frosting.

CHIFFON CAKE—P

Serves twelve to fourteen.

Chocolate Chip

In small mixing bowl, combine:	**2 cups all-purpose flour**
	1 3/4 cups sugar
	3 t. baking powder
	1 t. salt
Make "well" and add:	**1/2 cup salad oil**
	7 egg yolks, unbeaten
	3/4 cup cold water
	2 t. vanilla
Beat with spoon until smooth.	
In large mixing bowl, beat until stiff peaks form:	**7 egg whites**
	1/2 t. cream of tartar
Fold in gently until just blended:	**Egg yolk mixture**
Fold in with a few strokes:	**3 squares grated chocolate**

Bake in ungreased 10-inch tube pan, 325° for 55 minutes, then at 350°, 10–15 minutes. When cake tests done, invert over soda bottle until cold. Frost with Chocolate Icing.

CHIFFON CAKE—P

Orange

In small mixing bowl, combine: **2 cups all-purpose flour**
1 1/2 cups sugar
3 t. baking powder
1 t. salt

Make a "well" and add: **1/2 cup salad oil**
7 egg yolks, unbeaten
3/4 cup orange juice
3 T. grated orange rind

Beat with spoon until smooth.

In large mixing bowl, beat until stiff peaks form: **7 egg whites**
1/2 t. cream of tartar

Fold in gently until just blended: **egg yolk mixture**

Bake in ungreased 10-inch tube pan, 325° for 55 minutes, then at 350°, 10–15 minutes. When cake tests done, invert over soda bottle until cold. Frost with Orange Icing.

CHOCOLATE CAKE (DEVIL'S FOOD)—P

Serves ten.

In large mixing bowl, combine: **2 cups all-purpose flour**
1 3/4 cups sugar
1/3 t. baking powder
1 3/4 t. baking soda
1 t. salt
2/3 cup cocoa

Add and beat 2 minutes:	**2/3 cup soft shortening**
	1 cup water
	1 t. vanilla
Add and beat 2 minutes:	**3 eggs**

Bake in two greased and floured 9-inch layer pans at 350°, 30–40 minutes.
While still warm, place chocolate peppermint patties between layers. Let cool and frost with Snowy White Frosting.

CHOCOLATE SYRUP CAKE—P

Serves eight. Quick and rich!

In mixing bowl, beat together:	**1/2 cup margarine**
	1 cup sugar
Add one at a time, beating well after each addition:	**4 eggs**
Add and beat:	**16-oz. can chocolate syrup**
	1 t. vanilla
Fold in:	**1 cup self-rising flour**

Bake in greased and floured 9 × 13″ oblong pan at 350°, 45–50 minutes. Cool and sprinkle with confectioner's sugar.

COFFEE CAKE

Blueberry—D *Serves nine.*

In bowl, combine:	**3/4 cup sugar**
	1/4 cup soft shortening
	1 egg
Stir in:	**1/2 cup milk**
Add and blend:	**2 cups all-purpose flour**
	2 t. baking powder
	1/2 t. salt

Fold in: **2 cups blueberries, well drained**

Spread batter in greased and floured 9-inch baking pan.

Sprinkle with mixture of: **1/2 cup sugar**
1/3 cup all-purpose flour
1/2 t. cinnamon
1/4 cup soft butter

Bake 375°, 25–35 minutes. Cut in squares. This recipe may be doubled and baked in a 9 × 13″ oblong pan.

COFFEE CAKE

French Orange—D *Serves twelve to fourteen.*

In mixing bowl, combine and beat: **1 cup butter**
2 cups sugar

Add: **1/2 t. vanilla**
2 T. grated orange rind

Add one at a time, beating well after each addition: **5 eggs**

Add alternately a mixture of: **3 cups cake flour**
1 T. baking powder
pinch salt and
3/4 milk

Spoon into greased and floured 10-inch tube pan. Bake at 350° for one hour. Cool in pan on wire rack for 2 minutes.

In sauce pan, heat until dissolved: **1/4 cup butter**
2/3 cup sugar
1/3 cup orange juice

Pour evenly over cake in pan while cake is still hot. Allow cake to cool thoroughly in pan before removing.

COFFEE CAKE

Sour Cream—D *Serves twelve to fourteen. Very rich, very good!*

In large mixing bowl, combine and beat:	**1 cup butter**
	1 1/2 cups sugar
Add:	**3 eggs**
Combine:	**3 cups all-purpose flour**
	1 t. baking soda
	2 t. baking powder
	pinch of salt
Add to bowl alternately with mixture of:	**2 cups sour cream**
	2 t. vanilla

Spoon into greased and floured 10-inch tube pan.

Sprinkle with mixture of:	**2/3 cup brown sugar**
	1/2 cup white sugar
	2 t. cinnamon
	1/2 cup chopped pecans or almonds

Bake at 325° for 1 hour. Let cool in pan before removing.

DOBOSCH TORTE—P

Serves sixteen.

In mixing bowl place and cream:	**1/2 lb. unsalted margarine**
	1 cup sugar
Beat in:	**4 eggs, lightly beaten**
Stir in:	**1 1/2 cups flour**
	1 t. vanilla extract

Stir until well blended.
The torte is composed of 7 cookie-like layers. You may bake as many layers at a time as you have 9-inch cake pans. The layers are baked on the UNDERSIDE of the cake pan.
Grease and flour the *underside* of a 9-inch cake pan. With a spatula,

spread batter over the underside of the pan to a thickness of 1/8 inch. Bake at 350° about 7 minutes, until it tests done. Remove from oven and cut off any batter that has dripped over the sides of the pan. Loosen layer from pan with spatula. Put cake rack over it and invert. Wipe pan with paper towel and grease and flour it again. Repeat baking process until done.

Put layers together with chocolate filling. Use rest of filling on sides of cake.

Filling

In sauce pan, combine: **1 1/3 cup sugar**
1/4 t. cream of tartar
2/3 cup water

Stir over low heat until sugar is completely dissolved. Turn heat to moderately high and boil without stirring until it registers 238° on candy thermometer or until a drop of syrup in cold water forms soft ball.

In mixing bowl, beat until thick and light (3–4 minutes): **8 egg yolks**

Pour hot syrup into eggs, continuing to beat for 10–15 minutes until mixture is thick and smooth. If you set bowl of egg yolks into larger bowl of ice cubes, the process will take less time.

Beat in: **1/2 cup dark unsweetened cocoa**
2 t. vanilla
2 cups unsalted margarine in small pieces

Refrigerate filling while you make the glaze.

Glaze

Place one of the cake layers on a cake rack set on a larger piece of tin foil.

In a small heavy sauce pan, place and mix together: **2/3 cup sugar**
1/3 cup water

Without stirring (important) cook until caramel becomes a golden brown, being careful not to burn it. Pour immediately over cake layer and with a greased knife mark glaze into 16 equal wedges, cutting through to the bottom of the glaze. This glazed layer becomes the top of the torte. Frost sides of cake with rest of chocolate filling and refrigerate until ready to serve. To serve, slice along lines previously marked on glaze. You can make the layers well ahead of time and freeze them. Defrost the layers the day before serving and assemble the cake.

FRUIT CAKE—D

Serves twelve to fourteen.

In mixing bowl, cream:	**3/4 lb. butter**
	2 cups sugar
Add:	**3 eggs, slightly beaten**
	2 t. vanilla
Combine:	**3 cups flour**
	1 1/2 t. baking powder
	1/2 t. salt
And add alternately with	**1 cup milk**
Add:	**1 box white raisins mixed with**
	1/2 cup flour
Fold in:	**1 cup chopped nuts**

Line bottom of 10-inch tube pan with waxed paper and grease the rest. Bake at 325° for 1 hour and 15 minutes.

FRUIT TORTE—P

Serves eight.

In mixing bowl, combine and beat:	**1/2 cup margarine**
	1 cup sugar
Add and beat:	**1 cup flour**
	1 t. baking powder
	pinch of salt
	2 eggs

Place in 9-inch spring form.

Cover entire surface with: **1 pint blueberries**
or
sliced pared apples
or
sliced pared peaches
or
combination of fruits

Sprinkle top with: **sugar**
lemon juice
flour, if fruit is very juicy
cinnamon

Bake at 350°, 1 hour. Best served slightly warm.

GENOISE—P

Serves ten or twelve. An elegant dessert!

In warm large mixing bowl, combine: **6 eggs, at room temperature**
1 cup sugar

Beat at high speed until mixture is very thick and lemon-colored and stands in stiff peaks.

Fold in with rubber spatula: **1 t. vanilla**

Fold in in 3 parts: **1 cup sifted cake flour**

Fold in mixture of: **1 t. grated lemon or orange rind**
1/2 cup margarine, melted and cooled

Fold gently until no streaks show in the batter.
Pour into three 8-inch layer pans which have been greased, lined with waxed paper and greased again. Pans should be two-thirds full. If necessary, use fourth layer.
Bake at 350°, 25 minutes or until cake tests done. Cool in pan 5–10 minutes, then finish cooling on wire rack. May be filled with Cognac Filling, or Orange Filling, and frosted with Mocha Frosting, or Apricot

Glaze. May be made in large jelly-roll pan, frosted, garnished and cut into petit fours.

HAZELNUT CAKE—P

Serves twelve.

Hazelnuts are easily available in health food stores.

In large bowl, beat for 10 minutes until thick and light yellow:	**6 egg yolks**
	1 whole egg
Gradually beat in:	**1/2 cup sugar**
	1 cup ground hazelnuts
	1/3 cup bread crumbs
In another bowl, beat until foamy:	**6 egg whites**
Add:	**1/4 cup sugar, 1 T. at a time**

Continue to beat until the whites form stiff peaks.
With spatula mix gently one-fourth of the whites into the hazelnut mixture. Sprinkle 1 teaspoon flour over mixture and gently fold in the rest of the whites.
Grease and flour a 10-inch spring-form pan. Pour batter into pan. Bake at 275° in the middle of the oven 35–40 minutes, until it shrinks away slightly from the sides of the pan. Immediately remove the rim of the spring-form and let cake cool on rack. Divide cake into two equal layers. Fill and frost.

Filling and frosting

In bowl, whip until it begins to thicken:	**1 1/2 cups non-dairy whipped cream substitute**
Add:	**1 T. sugar**
	1 t. vanilla

Continue to whip until it forms peaks.
Place cake layer on serving dish. Slip 3 × 5″ pieces of waxed paper 1

inch under cake layer. This makes the paper easily removable when you are through frosting it and it also keeps the plate clean. Spread a 1/2-inch layer of filling on top of bottom layer. Place second cake layer over it and frost entire cake. Scatter 1/3 cup ground hazelnuts on the waxed paper segments. Lift paper gently and toss nuts onto cake. Repeat until all the nuts are used and remove paper. Refrigerate until ready to serve.

HONEY CAKE—P

Serves ten or twelve.

In large mixing bowl, beat until thick and lemon-colored:	**3 eggs**
	1 cup sugar
Mix together and add to eggs:	**1 cup strong coffee**
	1 cup honey
	2 t. allspice
	1 t. ginger
	1 t. almond
	1 t. baking soda
	1/4 cup salad oil
Fold in:	**3 cups all-purpose flour**
	1/2 cup raisins
	1/2 cup maraschino cherries, cut up

Pour into 9 × 13″ greased and floured pan. Decorate with slivered almonds. Bake at 350°, 1 hour.

ORANGE CAKE—P

A delightful cake!
Serves ten.

In large mixing bowl, beat well:	**3/4 cup shortening**
	1 1/2 cups sugar
Add and beat:	**3 egg yolks**

Combine: **2 1/4 cups cake flour**
1/2 t. salt
3 1/2 t. baking powder
And add alternately with: **3/4 cup cold water**
1/4 cup orange juice
1 T. grated orange rind
Fold in: **3 egg whites, beaten stiff**

Bake in two waxed-paper-lined 9-inch layer cake pans at 350°, 30–35 minutes.
When cooled, may be put together with Orange Filling and frosted with Orange Frosting.

PINEAPPLE UPSIDE-DOWN CAKE—P

Serves eight.

In 10-inch skillet or baking dish, melt: **1/3 cup margarine**
Sprinkle evenly over melted margarine: **1/2 cup brown sugar**
Arrange in pattern on margarine-sugar coating: **slices of canned pineapple**
maraschino cherries
pecan halves

Make cake batter and pour over fruit.

In mixing bowl, beat until thick and lemon-colored: **2 eggs**
Beat in gradually: **2/3 cup sugar**
Beat in all at once: **6 T. pineapple juice**
1 t. vanilla
Add: **1 cup flour**
1/3 t. baking powder
1/4 t. salt

Bake at 350°, 45 minutes. Turn out immediately, upside-down on serving plate. Do not remove pan for a few minutes, so that brown-sugar mixture runs down over cake. Serve warm.

POUND CAKE—P

Serves fourteen or sixteen.

In large bowl, beat until foamy:	**8 egg whites** **1/4 t. salt**
Add:	**1 cup sugar, 1/4 cup at a time**

Beat until it forms soft peaks.

In second large bowl, beat 5 minutes:	**2 cups margarine** **1 cup sugar**
Beat in until light and fluffy:	**8 egg yolks**
Add and continue beating until smooth:	**1 T. grated orange peel** **2 T. grated lemon peel** **2 T. lemon juice** **2 T. water**
Add 1/3 at a time:	**3 cups all-purpose flour** **1 t. baking powder** **1 t. salt**

Beat at low speed just until combined.
Fold in egg whites, 1/2 at a time. Do not overfold.
Pour batter into greased and floured 10-inch tube pan. Bake at 350° in middle of oven 1 hour or until cake tests done. Cool on rack 15 minutes. Turn out of pan and cool and glaze.

Glaze

Blend until smooth:	**1 T. margarine** **1 lb. confectioner's sugar** **1 t. grated lemon peel** **1/3 cup lemon juice**

Cake may be frozen unglazed. When defrosted, you may glaze it or sprinkle it with confectioner's sugar.

PUMPKIN CAKE—P

Serves twelve to fourteen.

In bowl, beat:	**1 cup sugar**
	1 cup honey
	1 1/4 cup salad oil
	1 1/2 cup pumpkin purée, canned
Add one at a time:	**4 eggs**
Fold in:	**1 1/2 cups whole wheat cake flour**
	1 1/2 cups white bread flour
	2 t. baking powder
	2 t. baking soda
	2 t. cinnamon
	1 t. salt
Stir in:	**1/2 cup dark raisins**
	1/2 cup light raisins
	or
	1 cup diced dried apricots
	1 cup chopped walnuts (save some for top)

Pour batter into greased and floured 10-inch tube pan. Bake at 350° in middle of oven for 1 1/4 hours or until cake tests done. Let cool until almost cold before turning out of pan.

SACHER TORTE—P

Serves six to eight.

In mixing bowl, beat well:	**1/3 cup margarine**
	6 T. sugar
Add:	**3 oz. (1/2 cup) semi-sweet chocolate bits, melted**
Add one at a time, beating well after each addition:	**4 egg yolks**
Stir in until no particles show:	**1/2 cup and 1 T. sifted flour**
Fold in:	**5 egg whites, beaten stiff but not dry**

Bake in greased and lightly floured 8-inch spring form cake pan at 325°, 1 hour and 15 minutes or until cake tests done. Let stand 10 minutes before turning out of pan. When cool, spread top of cake with 2 1/2 T. apricot jam. Pour Chocolate Icing over cake and spread quickly to coat top and sides.

SPONGE CAKE

Serves ten to twelve.

A.—P

In mixing bowl, beat until thick and lemon colored:	**6 eggs**
Beat in:	**1 cup sugar**
Fold in:	**1 cup flour**
	1 t. baking powder
	1 t. vanilla
	speck salt

Bake in ungreased 10-inch tube pan at 350°, 1 hour. Invert pan over soda bottle and let hang until cold.

B.—D

In large mixing bowl, beat until thick, lemon colored, and stands in peaks:	**4 eggs**
	1 cup sugar
Combine:	**1 1/2 cups flour**
	1 1/2 t. baking powder
	pinch of salt
And add alternately with:	**1/2 cup lukewarm milk**
	1 t. vanilla

Bake in ungreased 10-inch tube pan at 350°, 1 hour. Invert pan over soda bottle until cold.

Small Pastries

APPLE STRUDEL—P

Serves ten to twelve.

In bowl, combine: **2 cups all-purpose flour**
2/3 cup melted shortening
4 T. orange juice
pinch of salt

Roll between two sheets of waxed paper into an oblong 15 × 6″. Remove top sheet of waxed paper and spread dough thinly with jam.

Down center of oblong, place: **4–5 apples, peeled and sliced**
Raisins
Nuts
Coconut
3 T. lemon juice
1/2 cup sugar
2 t. cinnamon
1/2 t. nutmeg

Fold ends over. Flip over onto greased cookie sheet, sealed edge down. Brush with melted shortening. Sprinkle with cinnamon and sugar. Bake

375°, 35 minutes. Cut when hot. May be frozen wrapped in aluminum foil and reheated in the foil. Serve warm.

APPLE STRUDEL—P

Serves ten to twelve.

Prepared phyllo dough is available in many areas and makes an unsurpassable crust for strudel. The unused sheets of dough may be kept refrigerated or frozen.

To prepare packaged strudel dough, unroll two sheets and place them on a large damp kitchen towel. Keep the unused portion carefully wrapped in another damp kitchen towel to avoid its drying and cracking. Brush unwrapped dough with melted margarine and sprinkle the double layer with bread crumbs. Spread filling along edge of dough and use the towel to roll it up, jelly-roll fashion. Place roll on lightly greased baking sheet.

Filling

In large bowl, place: **4 large cooking apples, peeled, cored and cut into 1/2" slices**

Add and combine: **3/4 cup sugar**
2 t. cinnamon
3/4 cup white raisins
1 T. grated lemon peel
3/4 cup ground almonds

Brush top of roll with melted margarine and sprinkle lightly with bread crumbs. Make a couple of slits on top of roll to allow steam to escape. Bake in middle of oven at 450° for 10 minutes. Reduce heat to 400° and bake for 20 minutes until strudel is brown and crisp.

APRICOT STRIPS—P

Four dozen.

In mixing bowl, beat together: **1/2 cup margarine**
1/2 cup sugar
1 t. grated lemon rind

Add one at a time, beating well after each addition:	**2 egg yolks**
Add:	**1 cup flour**
	1/2 t. salt
	1/4 t. baking soda

Spread dough in greased 9 × 13″ pan.

Cover with:	**1 1/2 cups thick apricot jam.**

Spread with meringue.

Meringue

Beat until stiff:	**2 egg whites**
Add:	**1/4 cup sugar**
Fold in:	**1/2 cup chopped nuts**

Bake at 350°, 45 minutes. Cool. Cut into strips. Sprinkle with confectioner's sugar. May be frozen.

BEIGNETS SOUFFLÉS—P

Makes eighteen.

In 2-quart sauce pan, bring to boil:	**1 cup water**
Reduce heat to low and add:	**1/2 cup oil**
	1/2 t. salt
	1 cup all-purpose flour

Cook stirring vigorously until mixture leaves side of pot and forms ball. Cool slightly.

Add one at a time, beating well after each addition:	**4 eggs**
Half fill a heavy sauce pan with:	**Salad oil**

Heat to 375°.
Drop rounded tablespoonsful of batter into hot oil. Fry about 10 minutes or until lightly browned and cooked through. Drain. Refrigerate or freeze.

If frozen, heat puffs at 350°, 15 minutes. If refrigerated, heat 10 minutes. Sprinkle with confectioner's sugar. Serve with sauces.

Sauces

Apricot

In sauce pan, simmer 20 minutes or until thick:	**1 12-oz. can apricot nectar**
	1/2 cup sugar
Add and heat 5 minutes:	**16 canned apricot halves**
	2 T. lemon juice

Refrigerate or freeze. When ready to serve, reheat.

Strawberry or Raspberry

In sauce pan, bring to boil and simmer 5 minutes:	**1/2 cup sugar**
	1/2 cup water
Combine:	**1 T. cornstarch**
	2 T. sugar syrup

Add to sauce pan.

Add:	**2 cups fresh or defrosted frozen strawberries or raspberries**

Cook, stirring until thickened. Cool.

Add:	**1 T. Kirsch, Cognac, or Grand Marnier**

Chill.

BIRD'S NEST COOKIES—P

Two dozen

In mixing bowl, beat until fluffy:	**1 cup margarine**
Add slowly and beat:	**1/2 cup brown sugar**

Add and mix well:	**2 egg yolks**
	1/2 t. vanilla
	1/4 t. salt
Fold in:	**2 cups flour**

Shape into 1-inch balls.

Roll in:	**2 egg whites, beaten**
	1 1/4 cups chopped nuts

Bake on ungreased cookie sheet at 350°, 5 minutes. Remove from oven. Make slight depression in center of each ball. Bake 8 minutes. Remove from oven, cool and fill centers with jam. May be frozen.

BLONDE BROWNIES—P

Three dozen. Easy, plentiful, and delicious!

In large sauce pan, melt:	**1/4 lb. and 2 T. margarine**
Remove pan from heat and add:	**1/2 cup brown sugar**
Add one at a time and beat well after each addition:	**3 eggs**
Add:	**2 2/3 cups flour**
	2 t. baking powder
	1 t. salt
	1 t. vanilla
Add:	**1 small pkg. chocolate bits (6-oz.)**

Spread in lightly greased 15 1/2 × 10 1/2″ jelly roll pan. Bake at 375°, 20 minutes. Cut when cool. May be frozen.

CHEESE SQUARES—D

Sixteen.

Combine and press into 9-inch lightly greased pan:	**12 graham crackers, crushed**
	1/8 lb. melted butter

In bowl, combine: **1 lb. cream cheese**
2 eggs
3/4 cup sugar
1/2 t. vanilla
1 T. maraschino cherry juice
few drops red food coloring

Pour into graham crust. Decorate tops with halved maraschino cherries. Bake at 350°, 25–35 minutes. Cut when cold. May be frozen.

CHOCOLATE BALLS—P

Four or five dozen.

In bowl, beat: **1 cup margarine**
1/2 cup sugar
Add: **1/2 t. salt**
2 t. vanilla
2 cups all-purpose flour
2 cups nuts, chopped
1 6-oz. pkg. semi-sweet chocolate bits

Refrigerate until easy to handle. Shape into 1-inch balls. Place on ungreased cookie sheet. Bake at 350°, 10–12 minutes. While cookies are warm, roll in powdered sugar. May be frozen.

CHOCOLATE BROWNIES—P

Three dozen.

In sauce pan, melt: **1/2 lb. margarine**
4 squares chocolate
In mixing bowl, beat: **2 cups sugar**
4 eggs
Add: **melted chocolate mixture**
2 t. vanilla

1 cup flour
1 cup nuts, chopped

Bake in 9 × 13″ pan at 350°, 30–40 minutes. Should be wet for moist brownies. May be frozen. May be double-frosted with Mint Icing and Chocolate Icing.

CHOCOLATE DELIGHT BARS—P

Four dozen.

In a bowl, combine and beat:	**1/2 cup margarine**
	1 egg yolk
	2 T. water
Stir in:	**1 1/4 cup flour**
	1 t. sugar
	1 t. baking powder

Press mixture into greased 13 × 9 × 2″ baking pan. Bake at 350° for 10 minutes. Sprinkle batter with 12-ounce package of chocolate bits. Return to oven for 1 minute. Remove from oven and spread chocolate evenly over surface.

In bowl, beat until thick:	**2 eggs**
Add and beat:	**3/4 cup sugar**
Stir in:	**6 T. melted margarine**
	2 t. vanilla
	2 cups chopped nuts

Spread over chocolate layer. Bake at 350° for 30–35 minutes. Cut into 1 1/2-inch squares.

DATE BALLS—P

Two dozen.

In bowl, beat: **1/2 cup sugar**
1 egg
1 T. shortening

Add: **1 pkg. dates, cut up**
3/4 cup coconuts
1/2 cup nuts, chopped fine

Form into 1-inch balls. Bake on greased cookie sheet at 300°, 10 minutes. While warm, roll in confectioner's sugar.

DATE BARS—P

Sixteen pieces.

In mixing bowl, combine until blended: **3/4 cup melted shortening**
1 1/2 cups flour
1 cup nuts, chopped
1 t. salt
1 1/2 cups oatmeal
1 cup brown sugar
1 t. baking soda

Put one-half in bottom of greased 8 × 8" pan. Spread with filling.

Filling

In sauce pan, cook until thick: **1 pkg. chopped dates**
1 cup water
1 cup sugar
1 t. vanilla

Cool. Cover with rest of crumb mixture and pat down. Bake at 325°, 45 minutes. Cool and cut. May be frozen.

FILLED COOKIES—D

Four to five dozen.

In large bowl, combine and cream:	**1 cup margarine**
	2 cups sugar
Add:	**2 eggs**
	1 t. vanilla
Stir in:	**1 cup sour cream**
Fold in:	**5 cups all-purpose flour**
	2 t. baking powder
	1 t. baking soda
	1/2 t. salt

Refrigerate until easy to handle (about 1 hour). On lightly floured surface roll about one-fourth of the dough to 1/8-inch thickness. Cut into 3-inch circles with lightly floured cooky cutter. Place rounds on ungreased cooky sheet. Place 1 teaspoon jam in center of circle and top with second round with center cut out so that the jam shows through. Press edges together with fingers or floured fork. Continue the process until all the dough is used up. Bake at 375° for 8–10 minutes until golden brown.

FROSTED TINTED COOKIES—P

Four or five dozen.

In bowl, combine and beat until creamy:	**1/2 cup shortening**
	1/2 cup margarine
	1 cup sugar
	2 egg yolks
Add and mix well:	**2 2/3 cups flour**

Divide into 3 parts:

1. Leave white, add 1/2 tsp. vanilla.
2. Tint pink with few drops red food coloring, add 1/4 tsp. almond.
3. Tint green with few drops green coloring, add 1/4 tsp. peppermint.

Take 1/4 teaspoon of dough and, using fingers, shape into balls, crescents, or sticks. Bake on ungreased cookie sheet at 350°, 7–10 minutes.

Cool. Dip one end, both ends or top of ball into Chocolate Icing. Then dip frosted part into chopped nuts, coconuts, chocolate sprinkles, or silver dragees, etc. May be frozen.

GRAHAM CRACKER SQUARES—D

Makes sixteen.

In bowl, combine:
18 graham crackers, crushed in blender
1/2 cup nuts, chopped
1 6-oz. pkg. chocolate bits
1 t. salt
1 t. baking powder
1 can condensed milk
1 t. vanilla

Bake in greased 8-inch square pan at 375°, 20 minutes. Cool slightly. Cut. May be frozen.

JELLY ROLLS—P

Serves ten.

In mixing bowl, beat: **4 eggs**
Add and beat until thick and lemon colored: **3/4 cup sugar**
Fold in:
3/4 cup flour
1 t. baking powder
pinch of salt
1 t. vanilla

Pour onto wax-paper-lined 15 1/2 × 10 1/2" jelly roll pan. Bake at 350°, 10–12 minutes or until cake tests done. Loosen edges and immediately turn upside down on towel sprinkled with confectioner's sugar. Quickly and carefully remove the waxed paper. Spread cake at once with soft jelly or jam and roll up. To make miniatures, start rolling at wide end. Roll over once and cut off strip. Repeat. Cut each strip of roll into 2-inch pieces. Sprinkle tops with confectioner's sugar.

LACE COOKIES—P

About four or five dozen.

These are very easy to make but look complicated and impressive.

In sauce pan, combine and heat: **1/2 cup margarine**
1/2 cup light corn syrup
2/3 cup light brown sugar

Bring to boil and immediately remove from heat.

Stir in: **1 cup flour**
1 cup chopped walnuts

Drop 1/2 teaspoon of batter on greased baking sheet. The batter spreads, so leave about 3-inch space around each cookie. Bake at 325° for 7–8 minutes. Do not allow to get too brown. Cool 1 minute before removing from pan.

Melt: **6 oz. package of chocolate bits**

Use fork to dribble melted chocolate over cookies. Place in refrigerator until icing is firm. May be stored in refrigerator or frozen.

LEMON DROPS—P

Three dozen.

In bowl, mix together: **1/4 cup soft shortening**
1/4 cup margarine
3/4 cup sugar
1 egg
2 T. lemon juice
1 T. water

Stir in: **1 3/4 cups all-purpose flour**
1 1/2 t. baking powder
1/4 t. salt
1/2 cup chopped nuts

Chill dough. Roll into 1-inch balls and bake on ungreased cookie sheet at 400°, 12–15 minutes. While still warm, roll in confectioner's sugar.

MANDEL BREAD—P

Forty pieces.

In mixing bowl, beat:	**4 eggs**
	1 1/2 cups sugar
Add:	**1/2 cup melted and cooled margarine**
Fold in:	**4 cups all-purpose flour**
	1 t. baking powder
	pinch of salt
	2 t. vanilla
	1 cup chopped almonds
	1/2 cup raisins
	1/4 cup maraschino cherries, drained and chopped

Divide dough into 4 parts. With floured hands, shape into strips and place on two ungreased cookie sheets. Sprinkle with cinnamon and sugar. Bake at 350° 20 minutes, or until lightly browned. Cool and cut at an angle into 1/2-inch slices. If to be frozen, do not cut until defrosted. When defrosted may be cut and freshened in the oven.

MARBLE BARS—P

Two dozen.

In mixing bowl, beat:	**1/2 cup margarine**
	6 T. sugar
	6 T. brown sugar
	1/2 t. vanilla
	1/4 t. water
Add and beat:	**1 egg**
Mix in:	**1 cup and 2 T. flour**
	1/2 t. baking soda
	1/2 t. salt
	1/2 cup nuts, chopped
Sprinkle over batter:	**1 6-oz. pkg. chocolate bits**

Spread on greased 9 × 13″ pan. Place in 375° oven, 1 minute. Run knife through batter to marbelize. Continue baking 12–14 minutes. Cool and cut. May be frozen.

MARBLE SQUARES—P

Makes sixteen.

In bowl, beat until fluffy:	**1/4 lb. margarine**
	1/2 cup sugar
Add and beat until well blended:	**3 eggs**
	1 t. vanilla
Mix in:	**1/2 cup all-purpose flour**
	1/2 t. baking powder
	1/2 t. salt
	1/2 cup nuts, chopped

Divide batter into 2 parts.

Add to one part:	**1/2 cup semi-sweet chocolate bits, melted**

Spread white batter in greased 9-inch square pan. Add chocolate batter by spoonfuls. Cover with 1/2 cup coconuts. Bake at 350°, 35 minutes. May be frozen.

MOCK STRUDEL—P

Two dozen.

In mixing bowl, combine:	**2 cups flour**
	2 t. baking powder
	6 T. sugar
	pinch of salt
Add and blend:	**1/2 cup shortening**
	2 eggs, slightly beaten

Divide dough into 3 parts. Roll each part thin on floured board. Spread with thin layer of jam and sprinkle with raisins, nuts, coconut. Roll up like jelly roll. Sprinkle with cinnamon and sugar. Place on greased cookie sheet and cut half way through at 1-inch intervals. Bake at 350°, 40 minutes or until brown. Cut through while hot. May be frozen.

MOLASSES COOKIES—P

Four dozen 2-inch cookies.

In bowl, mix together:	**1/4 cup soft shortening**
	1/2 cup sugar
	1 egg
	1/2 cup molasses
Stir in:	**1 t. baking soda dissolved in**
	1/2 cup hot water
Stir in:	**2 cups all-purpose flour**
	1/2 t. salt
	1 t. ginger
	1/2 t. nutmeg
	1/2 t. cloves
	1/2 t. cinnamon
	1 cup raisins

Chill dough. Drop rounded teaspoonfuls about 2 inches apart on lightly greased baking sheet. Bake at 400° until set, 8–10 minutes. While slightly warm, frost with Quick Icing. May be frozen.

NEAPOLITAN COOKIES—P

Eight or nine dozen.

These cookies give a three-layer effect and add an interesting variation of color to a platter of cookies.

Dark Dough

In bowl, cream:	**1 cup margarine**
	1 1/2 cups brown sugar

Add and beat until light and fluffy: **2 eggs**

Mix in: **3 cups all-purpose flour**
1/4 t. salt
1 t. baking soda
1/2 t. cinnamon
1/2 t. ground cloves

Fold in: **1 cup coarsely ground nuts**
1 6-oz. pkg. chocolate bits

Light Dough

In bowl, cream: **1/2 cup margarine**
3/4 cup sugar

Add and beat until light and fluffy: **1 egg**
1 t. vanilla
1/2 t. almond flavoring
2 T. water

Mix in: **2 cups all-purpose flour**
1/2 t. salt
1/4 t. baking soda

Fold in: **3/4 cup raisins**
12 candied cherries, chopped

To assemble, pack one half of dark dough into waxed-paper-lined 10 × 5 × 3″ loaf pan. Pack in all of light dough, then remaining dark. Refrigerate 24 hours. To bake, cut dough lengthwise into thirds. Slice crosswise into 1/4 inch slices. Place 1 inch apart on ungreased cold cookie sheet. Bake at 375°, 8–10 minutes.

PINEAPPLE LAYER BARS—P

Two dozen.

In mixing bowl, beat until fluffy: **1/2 cup margarine**
1 cup sugar

Add: **3 eggs, slightly beaten**

Combine: **2 1/2 cups flour**
2 1/2 t. baking powder
and add alternately with: **1/2 cup pineapple juice**

Spread half batter in greased 13 × 9″ pan.

Spread with: **small can crushed pineapple, drained**

Cover with rest of batter. Sprinkle with topping.

Topping

2 T sugar
2 T melted margarine
2 t cinnamon
1/2 cup nuts, chopped

Bake at 350°, 40–50 minutes. Cool and cut. May be frozen.

RAISIN GINGER SNAPS—P

Three dozen.

In bowl, beat: **3/4 cup margarine**
1 cup sugar
1 egg
Blend in: **1/4 cup molasses**
Stir in: **2 1/4 cups flour**
2 t. baking soda
1 t. salt
1 t. ginger
1/2 t. cinnamon
1/4 t. cloves
1 1/2 cups raisins

Chill dough for about 1 hour. Shape into 1 1/2-inch balls. Bake on lightly greased cooky sheet at 350°, 8–10 minutes. Remove to cooling rack.

RASPBERRY BARS—P

Five dozen.

In bowl, combine:	**1 cup flour**
	1 t. baking powder
	pinch of salt
Add and beat until smooth:	**1/2 cup margarine**
	1 egg, beaten
	1 T. dairy substitute

Spread in lightly greased 10 × 15″ pan. Moisten hands and pat out. Spread with thin layer of raspberry jam. Spread topping over jam.

Topping

1/8 cup margarine, melted
1 cup sugar
1 1/2 cups coconut
1 egg, beaten

Bake at 325°, 25 minutes. Cut while warm and remove immediately from pan. May be frozen.

SARAH'S SOUR CREAM ROLL-UPS—D

Three to four dozen.

In mixing bowl, combine:	**2 1/2 cups flour**
	1/2 cup sugar
	2 t. baking powder
	1/2 cup shortening
	rind of 1 lemon
Add and blend:	**1/2 cup sour cream mixed with**
	1 t. soda
	juice of 1 lemon
	1 egg, beaten
	1/2 t. vanilla

Divide dough into 6 parts. Roll out thin on floured board. Spread with thin layer of jam. Roll up like jelly roll. Place on ungreased baking sheets and cut half way through at 1-inch intervals. Bake at 350°, 20 minutes or until lightly brown. Cool and ice.

Icing

1 T. sour cream
1/2 t. almond
confectioner's sugar enough for spreading consistency

Divide into 2 parts. Tint one part pink with few drops red food coloring. Tint other half pale green with a few drops of green coloring.

SCOTCH TOFFEE—P

Sixteen pieces.

In bowl, combine: **1/3 cup margarine**
2 cups instant rolled oats
1/2 cup brown sugar
1/4 cup dark corn syrup
1/2 t. salt
1 1/2 t. vanilla

Pack mixture into well-greased 8-inch square pan and bake at 450°, 12 minutes. Cool bottom of pan and remove from pan.

Spread with layer of: **6-oz. pkg. chocolate bits, melted**
Sprinkle with: **1/2 cup chopped nuts**

STRUDEL—P

Six or seven dozen.

In mixing bowl, place: **2 1/2 cups flour**
Make a "well" and add: **1 egg, beaten well**
1/2 cup oil

	1/2 cup lukewarm water
	1 t. sugar

Mix together with wooden spoon.
Divide dough into 6 pieces and roll each piece on *lightly floured* board. Brush with oil. Spread with filling. Sprinkle with bread crumbs. Roll as for jelly roll. Brush top with oil. Cut half way through at 1-inch intervals and sprinkle with cinnamon and sugar.

Filling

In bowl, combine:	**1/2 jar raspberry jam**
	1/2 jar orange marmalade
	1/2 jar apple jam
	3/4 box white raisins
	1/4 box dark raisins
	1/4 cup nuts
	1/4 cup coconut
Grate with rind and add:	**2 t. cinnamon and sugar**
	1 lemon
	1 orange
	1 apple

Place rolls on ungreased cookie sheet and bake at 350°, 30 minutes, until golden brown. Slide onto board and cut through.

TAIGLACH—P

Thirty-six pieces.

In mixing bowl, place:	**2 1/2 cups sifted flour**
	1/8 t. salt
	1 t. baking powder
Make a "well" and add:	**4 eggs**
	1/4 cup oil
	1 t. almond
Add (optional):	**1/2 cup raisins**
	1/2 cup nuts, crushed

Mix together with wooden spoon. Break off one teaspoon of dough and roll with floured hands into pencil-thick strips. Tie into a knot and tuck ends under.

Drop knots of dough into boiling syrup made of:

1 jar honey (1 lb.)
1 cup sugar
1/2 cup water

Cover and cook 20 minutes or until browned. Pour into side of pot 3/4 cup boiling water. Stir in 1 teaspoon ginger. Store in syrup in covered container.

THUMBPRINT COOKIES—P

Two dozen.

In mixing bowl, combine:

1/2 cup margarine
1/2 t. salt
1 t. vanilla
1/2 cup brown sugar
1 1/2 cups flour
2 T. dairy substitute
1/4 cup chocolate bits, chopped

Roll into 1 inch balls and make indentation in center of cookie. Bake on ungreased cookie sheet at 375°, 10–12 minutes. While hot, roll in confectioner's sugar. When cool, fill indentation with chocolate filling.

Filling

3/4 cup chocolate bits, melted with
1 T. shortening

Stir and cool slightly.

Blend in:

2 T. light corn syrup
1 T. water
1 t. vanilla

TRIPLE CHOCOLATE SQUARES—D

Thirty-five squares.

These squares take a little effort but are well worth it. You can make them ahead one day when you're in the mood for fussing and freeze them until you are ready to serve and savor them.

In bowl, combine and cream:	**3/4 cup margarine, unsalted**
	1/4 cup sugar
Add:	**3 squares unsweetened chocolate, melted**
Beat in:	**4 egg yolks, one at a time**
In another bowl, beat until foamy:	**4 egg whites**
	pinch of salt
Add:	**1/4 cup sugar**

Beat until it forms stiff peaks.
With spatula, stir one third of whites into chocolate mixture, then pour chocolate mixture over rest of whites. Sprinkle 1/2 cup flour over top and gently fold into mixture. Pour onto greased and floured jelly roll pan (11 × 17″). Bake at 350° in middle of oven, 15–18 minutes, until done. Turn cake onto rack to cool. When cool, cut cake in half to make 2 layers, each 8 1/2 inches wide. Over one layer spread filling 2 inches thick. Set second layer on top and refrigerate on rack for about 1 hour.

Filling

In sauce pan, combine:	**1 1/2 cup heavy cream**
	12 oz. semi-sweet chocolate bits

Stir over medium heat until chocolate dissolves. Reduce heat to simmer. Continue simmering stirring constantly until mixture thickens into a heavy cream. Pour into bowl and refrigerate for at least 1 hour. When mixture is very cold, pour in:

4 T. dark rum
1 t. vanilla

Beat until filling is smooth and creamy and forms soft peaks. Do not overheat or the cream will turn to butter.

Glaze

In sauce pan, combine: **1 cup sugar**
1/3 cup water
6 oz. semi-sweet chocolate bits

Heat over medium heat stirring constantly until the sugar and chocolate are dissolved. Remove pan from heat, cover, and let the glaze cool for about 20 minutes.

Set rack with cake on it over piece of tin foil. Pour glaze over cake. Refrigerate again on rack until the glaze is firm. Cut into 35 pieces, using sharp knife dipped in warm water.

TRIPLE CHOCOLATE SQUARES
Variation for Pareve

The cake and the glaze are pareve as they are. Only the filling needs to be adapted.

Filling

Melt and cool: **12 oz. semi-sweet chocolate bits**
In bowl, whip until thick: **1 1/2 cups non-dairy whipped cream substitute**
Whip until it forms peaks. Fold in: **Cooled chocolate**
4 T. dark rum
1 t. vanilla

Frostings and Fillings

APRICOT GLAZE—P

In sauce pan, boil together: **1 jar apricot preserves, strained**
2 T. sugar

CARAMEL ICING—P

Enough for tops and sides of two 9-inch layers.

In sauce pan, heat together: *** 1/3 cup caramel mixture (see recipe for Caramel Cake)**
6 T. margarine

Gradually stir in: **3 cups confectioner's sugar**

Beat until smooth and of spreading consistency. Add a little boiling water if mixture becomes too thick.

*If making frosting for cake other than Caramel Cake, caramelize 2 tablespoons sugar according to directions and add enough boiling water to make 1/3 cup liquid.

CHOCOLATE FROSTING—P

Enough for tops and sides of two 9-inch layers.

#1. In mixing bowl, combine and beat to spreading consistency:	**2 2/3 cups confectioner's sugar**
	1/3 t. salt
	4 T. cocoa
	1 egg yolk
	1/3 cup soft shortening
	About 5 T. hot water
#2. In mixing bowl, combine and beat to spreading consistency:	**2 cups confectioner's sugar**
	1/3 t. salt
	1 egg
	1/3 cup soft shortening
	2 squares chocolate, melted

CHOCOLATE ICING—P

Enough to pour over top of cake.

In sauce pan, melt together:	**1 square unsweetened chocolate**
	1 t. margarine
Blend in and beat only until smooth:	**2 T. boiling water**
	1 cup confectioner's sugar

COGNAC FILLING—P

Enough for four layers.

In small sauce pan, heat to boiling, stirring only until sugar dissolves:	**2/3 cup sugar**

1/8 t. cream of tartar
1/3 cup water

Continue boiling without stirring until mixture forms soft ball or registers 240° on candy thermometer. Cool slightly.

Beat: **5 egg yolks**

Pour syrup over egg yolks. Continue beating until mixture is cool.

Add: **1 cup soft margarine, 1 T. at a time**
1 T. cognac

Chill until firm enough to spread. Add small amount of confectioner's sugar to stiffen further.

CONFECTIONER'S SUGAR ICING

Enough to pour over top of cake.

#1.-**D** In bowl, combine: **1 cup confectioner's sugar**
1–2 T. milk or sour cream
1/2 t. vanilla or lemon juice

#2.-**P** In bowl, combine: **1 cup confectioner's sugar**
1–2 T. warm water
1/2 t. vanilla or lemon juice

*May be tinted any color with a few drops of vegetable food coloring. For Mint Icing, tint it green and substitute 1/4 t. mint flavoring for vanilla.

CREAMY FROSTING—P

Enough for two 9-inch layers.

In bowl, combine: **3 cups confectioner's sugar**
1/3 cup soft margarine
3 T. orange or lemon juice
1 T. grated rind

Beat until smooth.

MOCHA FROSTING—P

Enough for tops and sides of four 8-inch layers.

In sauce pan, melt: **6 oz. semi-sweet chocolate with 1/4 cup extra strong hot coffee**

Add and beat until mixture is smooth: **4 egg yolks**
3 T. confectioner's sugar
2/3 cup soft margarine

Chill to spreading consistency.

ORANGE FILLING—P

Enough for center of 8- or 9-inch cake.

In sauce pan over medium heat, combine and cook until thick: **1/4 cup cornstarch**
1 cup sugar
1/2 t. salt
1 1/2 T. lemon juice
1 cup orange segments, chopped
2 T. orange rind, grated

Remove from heat and add: **2 T. margarine**

Cool before spreading on cake.

ORANGE FROSTING—P

Enough for top and sides of two 9-inch layers.

In sauce pan, cook to thread stage, 232°: **3/4 cup sugar**
1/4 cup water

In small mixing bowl, beat until frothy: **2 egg whites**

Continue beating and pour hot syrup over whites. When mixture forms peaks,

Add and beat until thick: **1/2 T. orange juice**

SNOWY WHITE FROSTING—P

Enough for top and sides of two 9-inch layers.

In sauce pan, heat to boiling point but *do not boil;*
2 egg whites
2/3 cup sugar
3 t. corn syrup
1/8 t. cream of tartar

Remove from heat and beat until it holds shape.

Fold in: **1 1/2 t. vanilla**

QUICK ICING—P

In a bowl, combine and blend until smooth:
2 cups confectioner's sugar
enough water or orange juice to make it easy to spread
1 t. vanilla or lemon flavoring

Pies and Tarts

PIE CRUST—P

Easy and never-fail.

2-crust Pie

In large bowl, place:	**2 cups all-purpose flour** **1 t. salt**
Cut in with pastry blender or fork:	**1/3 cup and 1 T. shortening**

Blend until all shortening is covered with flour.

Cut in:	**1/3 cup and 1 T. more shortening**

Blend in until all shortening is covered with flour.

Sprinkle with:	**4 T. water, 1 T. at a time**

Mix lightly with fork until all flour is moistened. Gather dough together and press into ball. Divide dough about in half allowing a little extra for top crust. Roll out 1/8 inch thick on floured board (the less flour you use, the flakier the crust). Roll circle 1 inch larger than pie pan. Fold pastry over in half and quickly transfer to pie pan. Unfold and gently fit pastry

into pan. Trim off excess dough to make it even around pan.
Roll rest of dough for top crust a little thinner than for bottom crust, large enough to extend 1 inch beyond edge of pan. Fill pastry-lined pan with desired filling. Fold in half and transfer to top of filling. Trim edges, leaving 1/2-inch rim of pastry beyond edge of pan. Fold extra edge of top pastry under edge of lower pastry. Seal thoroughly by pressing together on edge of pan. Build up fluted edge by pinching pastry between thumbs and forefingers. Slit top crust in several places to allow steam to escape. Bake as directed.

1-crust Pie

Follow recipe for 2-crust pie cutting recipe in half. When you transfer bottom crust to pan, leave 1/2-inch rim of pastry to fold back and under. Build up high fluted edge as described above. Moisten rim of pie plate to prevent shrinking. Prick entire surface, sides and bottom, to prevent puffing. Bake at 475°, 8 minutes.

APPLE PIE—P

9-inch pie.
Serves eight to ten.

In bowl, combine:
3 lbs. baking apples, peeled, cored, and sliced thin
3/4–1 cup sugar to taste
1 t. cinnamon or nutmeg
Juice of half lemon if desired

Heap up in pastry-lined pan.

Dot with: **1 1/3 T. margarine**

Cover with top crust.

Brush crust with mixture of:
1/2 cup sugar
2 t. water (mixture should be thick)

Do not brush mixture on fluted edge. Bake at 450°, 10 minutes, then 350°, 40 minutes or until brown.

BAVARIAN PIE À LA JOFTES—D

Crust

In 8-inch pie plate, place:	**1 1/4 cups chocolate wafers (25)**
Combine with:	**1/2 cup butter, melted**

Mix well and pat evenly over bottom and sides of pie plate. Refrigerate.

Filling

In 1/4 cup cold water, dissolve:	**1 T. unflavored gelatin**
In sauce pan, combine:	**3 egg yolks, slightly beaten**
	1/2 cup sugar
	1/4 t. salt
Add slowly:	**1 cup scalded milk**

Cook, stirring constantly, until mixture coats spoon. Stir in dissolved gelatin. Cool.

Fold in:	**1 1/2 t. almond flavoring**
	3 egg whites stiffly beaten
	1/2 pint heavy cream, whipped
	few drops green food coloring

Pour into prepared chocolate pie crust. Refrigerate. When set, garnish with chocolate shavings.

Variation

Substitute for almond flavoring 1 1/2 t. vanilla, and tint pink. Garnish with chopped pistachio nuts.

BLUEBERRY PIE—P

9-inch pie.
Serves eight to ten.

Make pie crust for 2-crust pie.

In colander, wash and drain:	**2 pints fresh blueberries**
Mix through blueberries:	**3/4–1 cup sugar to taste**

1 t. cinnamon
juice of half lemon if desired
3 T. all-purpose flour

Heap up in pastry-lined pie pan.

Dot with: **1 1/3 T. margarine**

Cover with top crust.

Brush crust with mixture of: **1/2 cup sugar**
2 t. water (mixture should be thick)

Do not brush mixture on fluted edge of pie.
Bake at 425°, 35–45 minutes or until brown.

CHEESE TARTS—D

Serves twelve.

Mix together and pat into 1 doz. paper-lined muffin cups:
16 graham crackers, crushed
1/2 cup margarine, melted
2 T sugar
1/4 t cinnamon

In mixing bowl, combine and beat until creamy:
1/2 lb. cream cheese
1 egg
1/4 cup sugar
1/2 t. vanilla

Drop 1 tablespoon filling into each muffin cup. Bake at 375°, 10 minutes. Spoon 1 tablespoon top quality canned Bing cherries or pineapple pie filling over cheese mixture. Refrigerate.

CHERRY PIE—P

9-inch pie.

Make pie crust for 2-crust pie.

In colander, wash and drain: **2 pints pitted sour pie cherries**
Mix through cherries: **1 1/3 cups sugar**
1 t. cinnamon
4 drops almond flavoring
3 T. all-purpose flour

Heap up in pastry-lined pie pan.

Dot with: **1 1/3 T. margarine**

Cover with lattice crust top.

Lattice Crust

Weave 1/2″ × 10″ strips of pastry criss-cross on waxed paper. Chill. Flip quickly over top of filling. Seal and finish edge. Brush strips lightly with water and sprinkle with sugar.
Bake at 425°, 35–45 minutes, until crust is brown.

CHIFFON PIE—P

Serves eight to ten.

Chocolate

In sauce pan, melt: **2 squares unsweetened chocolate, grated**
in 1/2 cup boiling water
Add: **1 T. unflavored gelatin, dissolved in**
1/4 cup cold water

Stir until gelatine dissolves.
Beat until light and add: **3 egg yolks**
1/2 cup sugar
Add: **1/4 t. salt**
1 t. vanilla

Cool.

Fold into chocolate mixture meringue of: **3 egg whites, beaten stiff with**
1/2 cup sugar

Pour into cooled baked pie shell. Chill until firm.

CHIFFON PIE—P

Mocha

Follow recipe for Chocolate Chiffon Pie, but use strong hot coffee instead of boiling water to melt chocolate.

CHIFFON PIE—P

Lemon

In sauce pan, combine and cook until thick: **4 egg yolks**
1/2 cup sugar
1/4 t. salt
1/2 cup lemon juice

Add: **1 T. unflavored gelatine, dissolved in**
1/4 cup cold water

Stir until gelatine dissolves.

Add: **2 t. lemon rind, grated**

Cool.

Fold into cooled mixture meringue of: **4 egg whites, beaten stiff with**
1/2 cup sugar

Pour into cooled baked shell. Chill until firm.

CHIFFON PIE—P

Raspberry or Blackberry

Follow recipe for Lemon Chiffon pie. Before folding in meringue mixture, fold in 1/2 cup fresh drained raspberries or blackberries.

CHOCOLATE-ALMOND TARTS—D

One dozen.

In sauce pan, melt:	**6 milk chocolate bars with almonds** **16 marshmallows** **in 1/3 cup milk**
Fold in:	**10–15 almonds**

Cool for 1 hour.

Fold in:	**1/2 pint heavy cream, whipped** **1 T. sugar**

Pour into paper-lined muffin cups into which Graham Cracker Crust has been patted. See Cheese Tarts. Chill.

CHOCOLATE PIE—P

9-inch pie.

In mixing bowl, beat until fluffy:	**1 cup margarine** **1 1/2 cups sugar**
Add:	**4 squares chocolate, melted and cooled** **2 t. vanilla**
Add one at a time, beating well after each addition:	**4 eggs**

Beat until thick and light-colored.
Spoon into baked and cooled 9-inch pie shell. Refrigerate. Garnish with slivered almonds.

FRENCH APPLE PIE—P

9-inch pie.

In large bowl, combine:	**3 lbs. baking apples, peeled, cored, and sliced thin**
	3/4 cup sugar
	1 t. cinnamon or nutmeg

Heap into unbaked 9-inch pie shell. Sprinkle with crumb topping.

Topping

In small bowl, combine:	**1/2 cup margarine**
	1/2 cup brown sugar
Cut in:	**1 cup all-purpose flour**

Bake at 425°, 50–60 minutes.

FRUIT TARTS—P

Eight tarts.

Make pastry for 2-crust pie. Roll out and cut into 8 circles to fit over back of individual tart pans or muffin cups. Prick well to prevent puffing. Lay pans upside down on baking sheet. Bake at 475°, 8–10 minutes.

Filling

Cook according to package directions:	**1 package vanilla pudding**
Substitute for liquid:	**juice from 2 cans or 2 boxes frozen whole fruit (blueberries, strawberries, peaches, bing cherries, apricots)**
	enough water to make 1 1/2 cups liquid
Add:	**1 t. lemon juice, cognac, kirsch, or rum**

While mixture cools slightly, make glaze.

Glaze

Cook until melted: **2 cups currant, apricot, or other bright jelly**
4 T. sugar

Brush baked tart shell lightly with glaze. Spoon 1/2 inch cooked filling into shell. Arrange fruit on top and spoon on glaze. Refrigerate.

KAHLÚA PIE—P

11-inch pie.

In double boiler, combine: **4 1/2 t. unflavored gelatine**
1/3 cup sugar
4 egg yolks
3/4 cup coffee liqueur (Kahlúa)

Cook, stirring, until thickened. Cool.

In large bowl, beat: **4 egg whites**
Add: **1/4 t. salt**
1/4 cup sugar

Beat until soft peaks form.
Fold into cooled coffee liqueur mixture.

Beat to stiff peaks: **1 cup non-dairy whipped cream substitute**

Fold into coffee liqueur mixture and pile lightly into baked and cooled pie crust.

LEMON MERINGUE PIE—P

9-inch pie.

Bake one 9″ pie shell and allow to cool slightly. Be sure not to let it get cold.

Filling

In sauce pan, combine and cook over moderate heat stirring constantly until mixture thickens and boils:	**1 1/2 cups sugar** **1/3 cup cornstarch** **1 1/2 cups water**

Boil 1 minute.

Slowly stir one-half hot mixture into:	**3 egg yolks, slightly beaten**

Add this to hot mixture in pan. Boil 1 minute longer, stirring constantly. Remove from heat.

Blend in:	**3 T. margarine** **4 T. lemon juice** **1 1/3 T. grated lemon rind**

Pour into baked pie shell and cover with meringue.

Meringue

In mixing bowl, beat until frothy:	**3 egg whites** **1/4 t. cream of tartar**
Gradually beat in:	**6 T. sugar, one T. at a time** **1/2 t. flavoring (optional)**

Continue beating until stiff and glassy and stands in stiff peaks. Pile meringue onto pie filling. Be careful to seal meringue to edge of crust to prevent shrinking.

Bake at 425°, 6 minutes until delicately brown. Watch carefully. Cool gradually on wire rack away from drafts.

LIME MERINGUE—P

9-inch pie.

Follow directions for Lemon Meringue Pie. Substitute lime juice and rind for lemon and omit margarine. Add few drops green food coloring, just to a delicate lime green.

LIME—PINEAPPLE PIE—D

9-inch pie.

In bowl, dissolve:	**1 package lime jello**
In:	**1 cup hot liquid (add enough water to pineapple syrup to make 1 cup)**
Add:	**1/2 cup cold water** **2 T. lemon juice**

Cool.

Add:	**1 pint vanilla ice cream**

Refrigerate until it begins to set.

Fold in:	**1 9-oz. can crushed pineapple, drained**

Pour into baked Graham Cracker crust.

Crust

In 9-inch pie pan, mix together:	**16 graham crackers, crushed** **1/2 cup butter, melted** **1/2 cup sugar** **1/4 t. cinnamon**

Mix well and pat evenly over bottom and sides of pie plate. Bake at 350°, 10 minutes.

PECAN CUPS—D

Two dozen.

Pastry

In bowl, combine and blend: **3-oz. package cream cheese**
1/2 cup margarine
1 cup flour

Gather into a ball and chill. Place 1 T. dough into each small cupcake cup and press into shape of cup.

Filling

In bowl, combine and beat well: **1 egg**
1 cup brown sugar
1 T. margarine
1 t. vanilla
dash of salt

Place 1/2 pecan on bottom of cupcake cup. Spoon filling over it. Place 1/2 pecan on top. Bake at 325°, 30 minutes. Cool slightly before removing from pan. Handle carefully.

PECAN PIE—P

9-inch pie.

Make pastry for one-crust pie. Do not bake.

In mixing bowl, combine and beat: **3 eggs**
2/3 cup sugar
1/3 t. salt
1/3 cup margarine, melted
1 cup dark corn syrup

Fold in: **1 cup pecan halves**

Pour into pastry-lined pan. Bake 375°, 40–50 minutes, until set and pastry is brown. Cool.

QUICK TARTS—P

Kosher-Pareve pastry shells for tarts are available in the market and make a beautiful and easy dessert. Fill them with a variety of fillings.

Chocolate

In sauce pan, combine and cook until thick: **1 package chocolate pudding**
1 1/2 cups coffee
2 T. rum

Pour into tart shells and garnish as desired.

Strawberry

Fill shell with large fresh strawberries. Glaze with melted currant jelly.

STRAWBERRY FLAN—P

9-inch pie.
Serves eight or ten.

In a bowl, place: **1 cup flour**
Make a well and add: **1/4 cup margarine**
1/4 cup sugar
2 egg yolks
1/2 t. vanilla

Work together with fingertips until smooth. Chill 1 hour. Roll out on floured surface and line 9-inch flan ring. Bake at 375° for 15–20 minutes until lightly browned. Cool.

Fill with: **1 pint hulled strawberries**

Brush with glaze.

Glaze

In small sauce pan, heat: **3/4 cup red currant jelly**

TARTS—P

Any pie filling may be used as tart filling. Follow recipe for tart shells as given in Fruit Tarts.

Desserts

ALMOND ROLLA CAKE—P

Sixteen or twenty servings.

Line two baking sheets with brown paper. Using a 9-inch cake pan as guide, trace 2 circles on paper on each baking sheet and spread them evenly with Almond Meringue.

Almond Meringue

In bowl, combine and beat: **5 egg whites**
pinch of salt

Beat until stiff but not dry.

Add gradually: **3/4 cup sugar, 1 T. at a time**

Beat until meringue is thick and smooth.

Fold in: **1/4 cup sugar**
1 t. vanilla
3/4 cup almonds, grated

Bake at 250°, 30 minutes or until set. With heavy spatula, remove meringues to flat surface to cool and dry.

Assemble the four layers of meringue with Chocolate Filling.

Filling

In top of double boiler, beat until foamy:	**4 egg whites**

Set pan over hot water.

Beat in gradually:	**1 cup sugar** **2 cups margarine** **8 oz. semi-sweet chocolate, melted** **3 t. cocoa**

Beat until thick and smooth. Remove from heat and let cool until firm enough to spread.
Cover top and sides of meringues with Icing.

Icing

In bowl, combine and beat until fluffy and of spreading consistency:	**2 2/3 cup confectioner's sugar** **1/3 t. salt** **3 egg yolks** **1/3 cup soft margarine** **1 t. almond flavoring**

Sprinkle with finely chopped toasted almonds. Refrigerate overnight.

APPLE CRISP—P

Serves six.

In bowl, combine:	**6 apples, peeled, cored, sliced** **1/2 cup sugar** **1/4 t. cloves** **1/2 t. cinnamon** **2 t. lemon juice**

Pour into greased 1 1/2-quart casserole.

In bowl, blend to crumbly consistency: **1/2 cup sugar**
3/4 cup flour
1/8 t. salt
6 T. margarine
1/4 cup chopped nuts

Sprinkle over apples. Bake at 350° for 1 hour, until crust is brown. Serve hot. If desired, may be served with whipped cream substitute.

APPLE SQUARES—P

Two dozen.

In large bowl, place: **3 cups all-purpose flour**
1 t. salt

Cut in with pastry blender or fork: **1 cup and 3 T. shortening**

Blend until all shortening is covered with flour.

Sprinkle with: **6 T. orange juice, 1 T. at a time**

Mix lightly with fork until all flour is moistened. Gather dough into ball. Divide dough in half. Roll out 1/8 inch thick on lightly floured board. Roll 1 inch larger than 15 × 10 1/2″ jelly roll pan. Transfer to pan. If dough breaks, press together with fingers. Spread with Apple Pie Filling. Roll dough for top crust a little thinner than for bottom crust. Lay over apple filling. Trim edges even with pan and seal by pressing together with floured fork. Cut into top crust to form 2 dozen squares.

Brush crust with mixture of: **1/2 cup sugar**
2 t. water. Mixture should be thick

Bake at 450°, 10 minutes, then 350°, 30 minutes, until brown. Serve hot. May be frozen and reheated. You may substitute Blueberry Pie filling using 5 tablespoonfuls flour instead of 3.

BABA AU RHUM—P

Serves eight. Babas made easy!

In bowl, combine: **1/2 cup margarine**
1 t. lemon rind, grated
Add: **2 cups cake flour**
2 t. baking powder
3/4 t. salt
1 1/4 cups sugar
Add: **2/3 cup apricot nectar**
1 t. vanilla

Mix until all flour is dampened and beat for 2 minutes at low speed of electric mixer.

Add: **2 eggs**

Beat one minute longer.
Pour batter into greased and floured 8 × 4″ mold.

Sprinkle with: **1/2 cup currants or raisins**

Bake at 350° about 55 minutes or until cake tests done. Cool 10 minutes and remove from pan.
Pour sauce over warm cake and let mellow several hours before serving.

Sauce

In sauce pan, combine: **1/2 cup sugar**
3/4 cup apricot nectar

Bring to the boil. Remove from heat and cool slightly.

Add: **1 t. lemon juice**
1/2 cup rum

BAKLAVA—P

Twenty-four pieces.

Bottom Crust

In a bowl, cream:	**1 cup margarine**
	1/2 cup sugar
Beat in:	**1 egg, lightly beaten**
	2 T. cognac
Stir in:	**1 t. grated lemon rind**
	1 t. grated orange rind
	2 1/2 cups cake flour
	1 t. baking powder
	1/4 t. salt

Press dough over bottom and 1/2 inch up sides of 14 × 10 × 2 1/2″ baking pan. Bake at 350° for 15 minutes or until lightly brown.

Filling

In bowl, beat for 10 minutes:	**8 egg yolks**
	1/2 cup sugar
Mix together and stir in:	**1 T. flour**
	1 t. baking powder
	10 oz. almonds, finely chopped
	1/2 lb. walnuts, finely chopped
	1 t. cinnamon
	1 t. almond extract
	2 t. cognac
In bowl, beat until stiff, not dry:	**8 egg whites**
Fold into egg-yolk mixture:	**1/3 cup melted margarine**
	beaten whites

Pour onto the baked bottom crust.

Topping

The topping consists of 8 layers of phyllo pastry, each layer brushed with melted margarine, using 2/3 cup of margarine.
Cut through layers of phyllo topping with sharp knife to make diamond-shaped serving pieces. Bake at 350°, 50 minutes until set and lightly

golden. While cake is hot, spoon over it the cooled syrup and let stand for 24 hours. May be kept at room temperature for several days.

Syrup

In sauce pan, combine: **3 cups sugar**
1/3 cup honey
1 1/2 cups water
2 slivers lemon rind

Bring to boil, stirring until sugar dissolves. Boil 2 minutes. Stir in 3 tablespoons lemon juice and let cool to room temperature.

BLUEBERRY OR APPLE BLINTZES—P

Makes 2 1/2 dozen.

Prepare and cook Blintze Crêpes as given in Appetizers.

Blueberry Filling

In bowl, combine: **1 1/2 cups blueberries**
3 T. sugar
1 T. cornstarch
1/8 t. nutmeg

Fill and roll as directed for Blintzes. Arrange in greased baking dish and brush with melted margarine. Bake at 425° until brown, about 20 minutes.

Apple Filling

In bowl, beat until stiff but not dry: **1 egg white**
Fold in: **1 1/2 cups apples, finely chopped**
4 T. sugar
1/2 t. cinnamon

Fill and roll as directed for Blintzes. Arrange in greased baking dish.

Sprinkle with: **3 T. margarine, melted**
3 T. brown sugar

Bake at 425°, 20 minutes.

BOURBON CAKE—P

Serves sixteen to twenty. Rich and good!

In bowl, cream: **1 lb. unsalted margarine**
2 cups sugar
12 egg yolks, beaten

Beat until light.

Soak: **4 dozen Italian macaroons in**
1/2 cup Bourbon

Beat into egg-yolk mixture: **4 squares unsweetened chocolate, melted**

Add: **1 t. vanilla**
1 cup chopped pecans

In bowl, beat until stiff, not dry: **12 egg whites**

Fold whites into chocolate mixture.
Line 10-inch spring-form pan around sides and bottom with split lady fingers. Alternate layers of soaked macaroons and chocolate in lined pan, ending with chocolate layer. Sprinkle crumbled macaroons over top to garnish. Chill overnight. Remove sides of pan and serve.

CHEESE TORTE—D

Twelve servings.

Crust

Grease 8-inch spring-form pan.

In pan, combine: **2 cups graham crackers, crushed**
1/2 cup sugar
2/3 cup margarine, melted

Press crumbs over bottom and part way up sides of pan.

Filling

In bowl, combine and beat: **3 8-oz. packages cream cheese, at room temperature**

1 cup sugar
4 eggs
2 1/2 t. grated lemon rind

Pour into Graham Cracker Crust and bake 350°, 35 minutes. Cool. Refrigerate overnight. Spread with topping.

Topping

In sauce pan, combine and simmer one minute:
1 pint blueberries or strawberries
1/4 cup water
1 T. cornstarch with 2 T. water
1/2 t. lemon rind, grated

Cool and spread over torte.

CHERRIES JUBILEE—P

Serves eight. Dramatic and delicious dessert!

In sauce pan, simmer:
3/4 cup currant jelly
1 large can pitted Bing cherries, drained

Put into chafing dish.

Pour into center of fruit, without stirring:
1/2 cup brandy at room temperature

At table, ignite paper straw and flame the brandy. Spoon over individual portions of water ice.

CHOCOLATE CUPS—P

Eight 2-inch cups.

In sauce pan, melt:
8 oz. semi-sweet chocolate
1 T. shortening

Cool slightly. Coat inside of paper nut cups with thin layer of chocolate and refrigerate or freeze to harden. When thoroughly hardened, peel paper alway carefully and fill.

Filling

Caramel

In small skillet, melt until medium brown:	**1/3 cup sugar**

Stir constantly.

Blend and stir until smooth:	**3 T. margarine**
	2 T. hot water
In sauce pan, combine:	**3 T. sugar**
	Pinch salt
	1 T. flour
	1/2 T. cornstarch
Stir in gradually:	**1/2 cup hot water**

Cook over low heat, stirring until mixture boils.

Blend in:	**caramel mixture**
Beat a little of this mixture into:	**1 egg yolk, slightly beaten**

Beat into hot mixture in sauce pan. Stir over low heat until mixture boils again. Boil 1 minute. Cool. Fill cups. Garnish with crushed pecans.

CHOCOLATE MOUSSE—P

Serves six to eight.

In mixing bowl, combine and beat until well mixed but not frothy:	**5 egg yolks**
	3 T. cognac or dark rum
Combine, cool slightly and stir in:	**8 oz. semi-sweet chocolate, melted in**
	5 T. water

In another bowl, beat: **5 egg whites, stiff but not dry**

Stir 3/4 of whites into chocolate mixture. Fold in remaining whites. Pour into individual glass dishes. Chill well.

CHOCOLATE ROLL—D

Serves six to eight.

In small mixing bowl, combine and beat until light and fluffy:	**7 egg yolks**
	1 cup sugar
Combine, cool slightly and fold in:	**8 oz. semi-sweet chocolate, melted in**
	7 T. coffee
Fold in:	**7 egg whites, beaten stiff**
	pinch of salt

Place mixture in jelly roll pan that has been greased, covered with waxed paper and greased again. Bake at 350°, 15–20 minutes. Cool 5 minutes. Cover with slightly damp cloth and cool completely at room temperature. Place in refrigerator 1 hour. Remove cloth carefully and sprinkle cloth with bitter cocoa. Place cake on cloth. Remove wax paper from top and spread with filling.

Filling

Soften 1 t. gelatin in 1 T. milk and dissolve over hot water.

In small bowl, whip until stiff:	**2 cups heavy cream**
Beat in:	**1/2 cup confectioner's sugar**
	cooled gelatin
	2 T. rum

Roll up very carefully like jelly roll. This cake will crack as it rolls, but don't worry. May be frozen.
Serve with your favorite fudge sauce.

COFFEE-MARSHMALLOW DESSERT—D

Serves twelve.

Line spring form on sides and bottom with 24 lady fingers.
Place large mixing bowl in pot of hot water.

In mixing bowl, combine and melt: **1 1/2 lbs. marshmallows**
1/4 cup instant coffee dissolved in water to make 1 cup liquid

Cool in refrigerator.

Stir in: **1 pint heavy cream, whipped**

Pour into spring form.

Frost with: **1/2 pint heavy cream, whipped**

CRÊPES SUZETTE—P

Twenty-four to thirty crêpes.

Dessert Crêpe

In bowl, beat with wire whisk: **4 eggs**
Add and beat until smooth: **1 cup sifted flour**
2 T. sugar
Add gradually and stir until smooth: **1 cup milk substitute**
1 cup water

Let batter stand 30 minutes. If it becomes too thick, thin with spoonful of water.
Heat 5-inch skillet and coat with margarine. Pour in generous tablespoon of batter and tilt pan immediately, so that the batter will spread over the entire bottom of pan. When top of crêpe is just set and bottom golden brown, lift edges with spatula and carefully turn crêpe over. Brown other side 30 seconds or until crêpe is cooked. *Do not overcook.* Slide crêpe onto wire rack. Cook remaining crêpes, repeating the process, and pile them on top of each other. Crêpes may be kept warm in 250° oven.

Sauce

In sauce pan, heat together: **3 T. Maraschino**
3 T. Curaçao
3 T. Kirsch
4 T. Sugar
4 T. margarine
4 T. water
1 t. grated orange rind

Pour sauce into chafing dish at table.

Add: **1/4 cup warm cognac**

Ignite straw and flame sauce. Add crêpes one at a time and using fork and large spoon, turn each crêpe over in sauce and fold into quarters. Serve immediately.

CRÊPES WITH CHOCOLATE FILLING—P

Make Dessert Crêpes as above and keep them warm.

Filling

In small mixing bowl set in larger bowl filled with cracked ice, combine: **3 eggs**
1 1/4 cups sugar
4 oz. chocolate, melted

Beat with wire whisk until light.

Add gradually and beat until thick and creamy: **1 1/2 cups soft margarine**

Put a generous tablespoonful of Chocolate Filling in center of each crêpe. Roll up crêpes and arrange them side by side in baking dish.

Pour over crêpes: **1 cup orange marmalade, heated**
Sprinkle with: **finely chopped walnuts**
heated brandy

Ignite brandy and serve crêpes flaming.

Dessert Pears—P

Serves 12. An elegant but simple dessert!

Preheat oven to 375°.

Peel, leaving the stems intact:	**12 medium Bosc pears**
As the pears are peeled, drop them into a bowl of:	**cold water** **juice of 1 lemon**
In saucepan, bring to the boil and simmer 5 minutes to make syrup:	**1 1/2 cups water** **3/4 cup sugar**

Arrange the pears on their sides in one layer in a baking dish.

Pour over the pears a mixture of:	**1 cup white port** **1/2 cup orange liqueur** **sugar-water syrup** **3 wide strips of orange rind, thinly pared**

Place baking dish over low heat on top of stove and bring to the boil. Remove from heat and cover baking dish with aluminum foil. Bake at 375° for 30 minutes.
Remove foil. Turn pears to other side, lifting them by stems. Replace foil and bake pears 20–30 minutes more or until tender. Carefully transfer pears by stems to a deep bowl.

Add:	**1/4 cup brandy**

Pour pan juices over pears. Let pears chill in refrigerator overnight.
To serve, carefully place pears upright in shallow dish. Serve with juice and pass bowl of slightly sweetened non-dairy whipped topping flavored with one tablespoon of brandy or orange liqueur.

FRUIT PLATES—P

#1. Arrange thin slices of canteloupe on attractive round platter. Place wedges of orange, skin side up, between the slices of canteloupe. Pile fresh large strawberries with stems in center of dish.
#2. Arrange thin slices of Honeydew on attractive round platter. Make slight groove in each honeydew slice and insert thin slice of lime, skin side up. Pile bunches of green seedless grapes abundantly in center.

FRUIT TORTE—P

Serves eight or ten.

Pastry

In a bowl, combine:	**2 cups flour**
	1/4 cup sugar
Make a well and add:	**2 egg yolks**
	1 hard-cooked egg yolk, mashed

Mix together with finger tips.

Mix in until smooth and pliable:	**1/2 lb. unsalted margarine, melted and cooled**

On lightly floured surface, shape dough into a roll 6 inches long and 2 1/2 inches wide. Wrap in waxed paper and refrigerate for at least 30 minutes.
With sharp knife, carefully slice pastry roll into rounds about 1/4 inch thick. Pat rounds and smooth the edges, and layer them so that they completely cover the bottom of a 9-inch-spring form cake pan. Be sure no empty spaces show between them. Stand the remaining slices around the sides of the pan pressing them down about 1/2 inch into the bottom layer to secure them to the base and to create a scalloped effect around the top. Refrigerate for 10 minutes. Prick the entire surface with tines of a fork without penetrating through to the bottom of the pan. Bake at 325° in the middle of the oven for 40 minutes until pastry is firm and lightly browned. Place on cake rack and let it cool completely before removing the sides of the pan.

Filling

In small bowl, place: **1 envelope unflavored gelatine**
Mix with: **1 1/4 cups warm fruit juice drained from canned fruit**

Stir until gelatine has dissolved completely. Let cool slightly. Brush bottom of pastry shell with gelatine and let set for 5 minutes to seal crust. Reserve small amount of gelatine to brush over fruit.

Arrange in attractive pattern of concentric circles over shell and fill shell to within 1/4 inch of top: **5–6 cups of fruits, fresh or drained canned**

Glaze final layer with thin coating of gelatine. If gelatine becomes too thick to brush smoothly, place bowl of gelatine in pan of warm water for a few minutes.

To decorate outside of shell, beat: **1 egg white until thickened slightly**
Sprinkle with: **1 T. sugar**

Beat until stiff peaks form.
Coat outside of shell with meringue and press 1 1/2 cups sliced almonds against it. The entire outer surface should be covered with almonds.

ITALIAN LOAF CAKE—D

Serves eight. This is what a dessert should taste like! Your guests will never guess how simple this is.

With sharp serrated knife, cut the end crusts off of a 9 × 3″ pound cake and level the top if it is rounded. You may use a bought pound cake just as effectively.

Cut cake into horizontal slices 1/2 inch thick.

In a bowl, combine and beat: **1 lb. ricotta cheese**
2 T. heavy cream

	1/4 cup sugar
	3 T. orange-flavored liqueur
Fold in:	**3 T. coarsely chopped candied fruit**
	2 oz. chocolate bits

Center bottom slab of cake on serving plate. Spread generously with ricotta mixture. Place another slab of cake on top and spread with more ricotta. Repeat until all the cake and filling have been used up, ending with cake layer on top. Press loaf together to make it even and compact. Refrigerate for about 2 hours, until cheese is firm. Frost.

Frosting

In sauce pan, melt:	**12 oz. chocolate bits**
	3/4 cup strong black coffee
Remove pan from heat and beat in:	**1/2 lb. unsalted butter, one piece at a time**

Continue beating until mixture is smooth. Chill until frosting thickens to spreading consistency. Spread frosting evenly on top, sides, and ends of cake. Refrigerate for at least 24 hours before serving, so that the cake mellows.

GLAZED ORANGES—P

Serves six.

Remove thin orange part of peel from:	**3 navel oranges**

Cut into very thin julienne strips.

In small sauce pan, place:	**orange-peel strips**

Barely cover with water and bring to boil. Simmer for 10 minutes. Drain and run cold water over the peel.

In sauce pan, place:	**1/2 cup water**
	2 T. honey
	1 1/2 cups sugar

Heat, stirring until sugar dissolves. Boil until syrup registers 230° on candy thermometer or spins thread in cold water. Immediately add the blanched peel. Stir gently. Let peel stand in syrup for 30 minutes.

Add:	**1/4 cup orange juice** **1/4 cup Grand Marnier**
Remove the remainder of peel and white pith from:	**6 navel oranges (you have only used the thin skin of 3 of the 6 oranges)**

Place oranges on shallow serving platter, top with peel, and spoon syrup over oranges. Chill well before serving. Baste often with syrup.
Serve on fruit plate with dessert fork and knife. It's very refreshing served after a heavy meal.

MARINATED PINEAPPLE—P

Cut thin slice off bottom of ripe pineapple. Cut frond end off, leaving fronds attached to use as a cover. When you're through, the pineapple will look whole. Using grapefruit cutter, carefully scoop out center cavity of pineapple. Remove core and cut pineapple into chunks. Place bottom slice on platter. Set shell on bottom slice. Refill with cut pineapple. Pour in generous amount of sweet white wine. Replace frond end. Surround pineapple with large fresh strawberries with stems. Refrigerate several hours.

PARIS CHOU—P

Serves eight or ten.

Brush one baking sheet with vegetable oil and dust lightly with flour. Using 8-inch cake pan as guide, trace circle on baking sheet and spoon dough for Chou in ring about 1 inch high and 1 1/2–2 inches thick inside guide marked on baking sheet.

Dough for Chou

In small sauce pan, combine and beat until boiling:	**1 cup water**
	6 T. margarine
	1/8 t. salt
Add all at once:	**1/8 t. salt**
	1 cup flour

Stir until mixture forms ball and leaves sides of pan. Remove from heat.

Beat in:	**4 eggs, one at a time**
Brush ring of dough with:	**1/2 egg, lightly beaten**
Sprinkle with:	**1/4 cup slivered blanched almonds**

Bake at 450°, 10–15 minutes, 350°, 10–15 minutes longer. With point of knife, pierce halfway down through ring at edge in several places to allow steam to escape. Bake 15 minutes longer, until shell is well browned and dry inside. Cool on wire rack.
When cool, split shell crosswise. Fill bottom shell and hollows in top shell with Praline Cream. Put 2 halves together.

Praline Cream

In small sauce pan, bring to boil:	**1 cup sugar**
	1/3 cup water
	1/4 t. cream of tartar

Boil without stirring until syrup reaches 240° and spins long thread when placed in cold water.

Gradually pour into syrup, beating constantly:	**4 beaten egg yolks**

Beat until mixture is very thick.

Beat in:	**1/2 lb. margarine, a little at a time**
Stir in:	**2 t. vanilla**
	1/2 cup Praline Powder

Praline Powder

In small sauce pan, combine, heat, and stir until sugar dissolves:
3/4 cup sugar
1/4 cup water
1/4 t. cream of tartar
1/2 cup blanched almonds

Continue to heat without stirring until syrup is color of dark molasses. Be careful not to burn. Pour immediately onto greased cookie sheet and allow to cool. When cool, break praline into rough pieces. Place 1/4 of pieces in blender and blend until pulverized, about 15 seconds. Repeat with remaining praline. Store powder in tightly covered jar.

PROFITEROLE—D

Serves eight. Great import from Great Britain! This is a dessert using cream puffs filled with flavored whipped cream over which you pour a delightful hot chocolate sauce. Serve the puffs in a large glass bowl and spoon into individual dessert dishes.

Use half the recipe for Cream Puffs. These may be made well ahead of time and frozen. When ready to use, defrost and fill with whipped cream filling.

Filling

In bowl, combine and chill for 1 hour:
1 cup whipping cream
4 T. confectioner's sugar
1 t. vanilla

When thoroughly chilled, beat until it is very stiff and holds its shape. Place filled puffs in bowl and pour hot chocolate sauce over them when ready to serve.

Chocolate Sauce

In sauce pan, melt:
3 squares unsweetened chocolate
5 T. butter

Remove from heat and add alternately: **3 cups confectioner's sugar with**
1 cup undiluted evaporated milk

Blend well. Bring to the boil over medium heat. Cook and stir for 8 minutes.

Stir in: **1 t. vanilla**

SOUFFLÉ—D

Serves six.

In bowl, combine: **2 cups apricot purée (junior baby food)**
juice of 1/2 lemon
4 T. apricot liqueur

Set aside.

In sauce pan, cook until thick: **3/4 cup milk**
1/4 cup cornstarch
4 T. sugar
pinch of salt

Remove from heat.

In bowl, beat: **3 egg yolks**

Spoon some of hot mixture into yolks. Pour combined mixture back into hot mixture.

Add: **1 T. butter**
1 t. vanilla

Pour over apricot mixture.

In bowl, beat until peaks form: **3 egg whites**
1/4 t cream of tartar

Fold into apricot mixture. Grease only the bottom of a 1 1/2-quart soufflé mold. Pour batter into mold. Set mold in pan of water. Bake at 325°, 1 1/4 hours. Top will be crusty and center soft. Spoon into dessert dishes to serve and pass a bowl of Chantilly cream.

Chantilly cream is fresh cream beaten to the consistency of a mousse, sweetened and flavored as desired.

Variation

Substitute 2 cups of mashed bananas for the apricots and use rum instead of the liqueur.

STRAWBERRY CAKE—P

Serves ten. Serve this beautiful cake in May, when strawberries first come out as a harbinger of summer.

Layers

In bowl, beat until thick and light:	**7 egg yolks**
Add:	**1 cup sugar, 1 T. at a time**

Continue beating until mixture becomes very thick.

Combine:	*** 1/2 cup shelled filberts, finely grated**
	1/2 cup pecans or walnuts, finely grated
	1/8 t. salt
	2 T. cake flour

Fold nut mixture into egg-yolk mixture.

In bowl, beat until stiff, not dry:	**7 egg whites**

Stir 1/3 of whites into yolk mixture. Fold in remaining whites.
Pour into two 9-inch layer pans which have been greased, lined with waxed paper and greased again. Bake at 350°, 35–40 minutes. Set cake pans on rack. Slide knife around edges of cake to loosen. Cool in pan for 10 minutes. The layers shrink. Remove from pans. Peel off waxed paper and let cool on rack.
*Filberts may be found at local health food stores. They are very tough nuts and should be grated in a Mouli grater, *not* in a blender.

Filling

In bowl, place:	**1 pint strawberries, sliced**
Sprinkle with:	**2 T. sugar**
	2 T. strawberry liqueur

Set aside.

In bowl, beat until thick:	***1 cup whipped-cream substitute**
Fold in:	**strawberry mixture**

Spread between cake layers.

*If desired you may use heavy cream in filling. (**D**). If you do, add 1 teaspoon gelatine combined with 2 tablespoons water, dissolved over heat. Add gelatine mixture to cream as it begins to thicken. Continue to beat until mixture is very thick.

Glaze

In small sauce pan, heat until it melts:	**12 oz. currant jelly**
Add:	**2 T. strawberry liqueur**

Brush jelly glaze over top of cake.

Arrange on top of cake, pointed side up:	**1 pint whole strawberries, hulled**

Spoon remaining glaze over strawberries.

Finishing

In bowl, beat until thick:	**3/4 cup whipped-cream substitute**

Spread around outside edge of cake.

Sprinkle over sides of cake:	**1/3 cup filberts, chopped**

Refrigerate several hours, or overnight.

STRAWBERRIES ROMANOFF—D

Serves six.

In large glass bowl, place: **1 qt. choice fresh strawberries, hulled**

Toss lightly to taste with: **sugar**
Cointreau
Kirsch

Refrigerate.

One hour before serving, place in refrigerator: **1 pint vanilla ice cream**

Whip: **1 pint heavy cream**

Fold in: **1/2 cup crushed almonds (optional)**

When ready to serve, combine whipped cream and ice cream. Fold in strawberries.
Bowl of strawberries may be used as centerpiece and creams folded in at table.

SURPRISE PUDDING—P

Serves six to eight. The surprise ingredient is sliced white bread.

Remove crusts from: **10–12 slices of white bread**

Cut one slice so that it conforms to the shape of the bottom of a 2-quart deep bowl or a charlotte mold. Set it in place. Trim 6 or 7 slices of the bread into truncated wedges (about 3 inches wide across the bottom and 4 inches wide across the top). Stand the wedges of bread, narrow end down, around inner surface of mold or bowl, overlapping them about 1/4″. Fill with fruit mixture.

Fruit mixture

In a bowl, place: **2 quarts fresh ripe raspberries, blackberries, or blueberries**

Toss lightly with: **1 1/4 cups sugar to taste**

Pour fruit mixture into mold and cover top completely with remaining bread. Cover top of mold with flat plate and on it set a heavy pan. Refrigerate for at least 12 hours, until the bread is completely saturated with fruit syrup. Unmold on to a plate and serve. You may pass a bowl of non-dairy whipped-cream substitute.

TRIFLE—D

Serves six to eight. A wonderful way to use up stale cake. You must use only stale cake.

Cut into 1-inch thick slices:	**1 5 × 4 × 3″ pound cake (stale)**
Spread slices with:	**4 T. raspberry jam**

Place 2 or 3 cake slices jam-side-up in bottom of glass serving bowl. Cut remaining slices of cake into 1-inch cubes and scatter them over the cake slices.

Sprinkle with:	**1/2 cup blanched sliced almonds**
Pour in:	**1 cup medium-dry sherry**
	1/4 cup brandy

Steep at room temperature at least 30 minutes.

In large chilled bowl, whip until thick:	**2 cups heavy cream**
Add:	**2 T. sugar**

Continue to beat until cream forms peaks.

To assemble:

Scatter over cake:	**2 cups fresh raspberries or**
	2 10-oz. packages frozen raspberries, defrosted and drained

Reserve 10 of the best-looking raspberries to garnish top.
Spread prepared and chilled vanilla pudding over berries. Spread whipped cream over pudding. Garnish with raspberries and 1/2 cup almonds. May be refrigerated for several hours.

VELVET CHOCOLATE CAKE—P

Serves ten. Serve small pieces—it's very rich!

In sauce pan, melt:	**1 lb. sweet baking chocolate**
	1 T. water
Remove from heat and stir in:	**1 T. flour**
	1 T. sugar
	10 T. margarine
In bowl, beat lightly:	**4 egg yolks**

Beat into chocolate mixture with wire whisk.

In bowl, beat until stiff, not dry:	**4 egg whites**

Fold into chocolate mixture.
Pour into 8-inch spring-form pan lined with waxed paper. Bake at 425° for 15 minutes. Turn off heat, open oven door, and allow cake to cool completely in oven. Garnish with non-dairy whipped-cream substitute.

Frozen Desserts

BAKED ALASKA

Serves twelve. May be made as far ahead as 2 weeks and kept in freezer.

#1.-**P** Line 9 inch pie plate with thin layer of sponge cake.
Line 2 1/2-quart mixing bowl with aluminum foil.

Pack with:	**1 qt. lime water ice**
	1 qt. raspberry water ice

Freeze immediately until very firm.
When *firm* invert into lined pie plate. Remove foil.
Cover completely with meringue. Be careful to seal meringue to edge of pie plate to prevent water ice from melting.

Meringue

In small bowl, beat until stiff:	**3 egg whites**
	pinch of salt
	1/4 t. cream of tartar
Add gradually while still beating:	**1/2 cup light corn syrup**
	2 T. marshmallow fluff

Beat until it stands in firm peaks. Bake in pre-heated 500° oven, 5 minutes. Watch carefully and turn in oven if necessary to brown evenly. Remove and place in freezer immediately. When time to serve, remove from freezer 1 hour ahead and place in refrigerator to defrost enough to cut. Serve with defrosted frozen strawberries. Cut into wedges with knife dipped in cold water.

#2.-**D** Line pie plate with Chocolate Crumb Crust.

In 9-inch pie plate, place:	**1 1/2 cups crushed chocolate wafers (28)**
Combine with:	**1/2 cup butter, melted**

Mix well and pat evenly over bottom and sides of pie plate. Refrigerate. Follow procedure described above, substituting 2 qts. ice cream (chocolate, vanilla, or coffee) for water ice. Do not use ice creams which have sauce whirled through them or chips in them, because they do not freeze firmly.
Cover with meringue and bake and freeze as directed above.
Serve with your favorite rich fudge sauce.

BISQUE TORTONI—P

Makes four quarts.

In sauce pan, combine:	**2 cups sugar**
	1/2 cup water

Bring to the boil and cook until syrup registers 236° on candy thermometer or forms soft ball in cold water.

In bowl, beat until very thick:	**8 egg yolks**
	1/4 t. salt
Add gradually while beating:	**syrup**

Continue beating until mixture forms peaks. Chill.

Fold in:	**6 cups non-dairy whipped-cream substitute, whipped**
	1/4 cup rum or cognac
Stir in:	**5 finely chopped almonds**

Turn into paper cups and freeze. Sprinkle with additional crushed almonds.

CHOCOLATE UPSIDE-DOWN DESSERT—D

Serves twelve. May be made two weeks ahead and kept in freezer.

In mixing bowl, combine:	**4 cups chocolate wafers, crushed**
	1 cup butter, melted

Set aside 2/3 cup of crumbs. Press remaining crumbs over bottom and up sides of 9-inch spring-form pan. Freeze about 15 minutes or until firm. Remove from freezer.

Spread over bottom of pan in even layer:	**1 qt. vanilla ice cream**
Sprinkle with:	**1/3 cup reserved crumbs**

Return to freezer until ice cream is firm.

Make 2nd layer by spreading evenly:	**1 qt. pistachio ice cream**
Sprinkle with:	**1/3 cup reserved crumbs**

Return to freezer until ice cream is firm.

Make 3rd layer by spreading evenly:	**1 qt. chocolate ice cream**

Cover top of spring-form pan with aluminum foil and return to freezer until needed. Ten minutes before serving, invert spring form onto chilled serving plate. Release catch and remove sides and bottom of pan. Garnish cake with ring of coconut flakes. To serve, cut into wedges with knife dipped in cold water.

ICE CREAM SOUFFLÉ—D

Serves eight.

In bowl, combine: **1 qt. vanilla ice cream, softened slightly**
4 macaroons, crumbled
3 T. Grand Marnier

Fold in: **1 cup heavy cream, whipped**

Spoon into 6-cup metal mold.

Sprinkle surface lightly with: **4 T. toasted almonds, chopped**
4 t. confectioner's sugar

Cover with aluminum foil and freeze until firm. Unmold when ready to serve by placing hot towel on mold for 4–5 seconds. Loosen edge with spatula and turn out on chilled dish.
Serve with Hot Strawberry Sauce.

Sauce

In sauce pan, simmer: **1 pt. fresh strawberries cut in half**
or
1 10-oz. package frozen sliced strawberries, thawed

For fresh berries, add: **1/8 cup sugar**

Remove from heat and stir in: **4 t. Grand Marnier**

MERINGUE SHELLS WITH ZABAGLIONE SAUCE—P

Serves twelve.

In bowl, beat until stiff: **6 egg whites**

Gradually beat in: **1 cup sugar**

Continue beating and add alternately: **1 cup sugar**
1 1/2 t. lemon juice or vinegar

Beat until very stiff and glossy. Drop by spoonfuls to make 12 circles on brown paper on baking sheet. Bake at 275°, 40 minutes, until delicately brown and crusty. Cool. Remove from pan. Place scoop of water ice on circle. Serve with Zabaglione Sauce, or with Brandied Fruit.

ORANGE-RASPBERRY BASKETS—P

Serves eight.

With sharp paring knife, cut in half: **4 large oranges**

Carefully squeeze out juice and scoop out pulp and reserve.

Place in blender, a little at a time: **3 10-oz. packages frozen raspberries**

Rub the raspberry purée through sieve to remove seeds.

Stir in: **1/4 cup orange juice**
1/8 t. mint extract

Pour into freezer tray and freeze until mushy. Remove from freezer and beat until smooth. Carefully spoon raspberry purée into orange shells, making tops fairly level. Freeze until *firm.* Frost orange shells with Meringue, sealing edges to rind.

Meringue

In small bowl, beat until stiff: **3 egg whites**
pinch of salt
1/4 t. cream of tartar

Add gradually, while still beating: **1/2 cup light corn syrup**
2 T. marshmallow fluff

Beat until it stands in firm peaks.

Fold in: **1 T. finely grated orange rind**

Place shells on baking sheet and broil quickly, until meringue is golden brown. Freeze immediately. When ready to serve, defrost one hour in refrigerator.

TANGERINE SURPRISE—P

Serves six.

With sharp paring knife, cut tops off: **6 tangerines**

With spoon, gently scoop out fruit sections. Reserve shells and tops. Remove seeds from sections and extract juice. Use enough additional tangerine sections (4–6 more tangerines) to make 2 cups of juice.

In sauce pan, combine and boil 5 minutes:
2 cups water
1 cup sugar
2 T. corn syrup

Add: **2 T. grated tangerine peel**

Cool.

Add:
2 cups tangerine juice
2 T. lemon juice
few drops red and yellow food coloring

Rub mixture through fine sieve. Pour into freezer tray. Freeze until mushy.

Fold in: **2 egg whites, beaten stiff with 2 T. sugar**

Freeze until firm. Fill each tangerine shell with ice. Cover each with tangerine top. Wrap with foil and return to freezer until ready to serve. Before serving, garnish each with sprig of mint.

CRANBERRY WATER ICE—P

Serves eight.

In sauce pan, cook until skins are broken (10 min.):
1 qt. cranberries
1 cup water

Rub through sieve to make smooth pulp.

Stir in: **2 cups sugar**
1/4 cup lemon juice
1 t. orange rind, grated
2 cups cold water

Pour into freezing tray. Freeze until firm, stirring 2 or 3 times. Freeze 2–3 hours. Serve in sherbet dishes with Pareve cookies.

FRUIT WATER ICE—P

Serves eight.

Soften 1 teaspoon gelatin in 2 tablespoon cold water.

In sauce pan, combine and stir over low heat: **3/4 cup sugar**
1 1/2 cups water

Boil 5 minutes.

Stir in: **gelatin**

Cool.

Stir in: **4 T. lemon juice**
1 cup crushed fruit (orange, lemon, pineapple or grape, pulp and juice)

Pour into freezing tray. Freeze to a mush. Beat in chilled bowl until fluffy.

Fold in: **1 egg white, stiffly beaten**

Return to freezing tray and freeze until firm, stirring occasionally.

LEMON ICE WITH FROSTED GRAPES—P

Serves eight.

Line 1-quart mixing bowl with aluminum foil.
Fill with Lemon Water Ice. Freeze until *firm.* Unmold on chilled serving dish. Remove foil.

Place directly on water ice: **1 pt. large, perfect berries or cherries**

Arrange around mold: **Clusters of blue, green, and red grapes, frosted**

Frosted Grapes

Pick over and wash grapes, dividing into small bunches. Sprinkle with sugar. Place in coldest part of refrigerator for 1 hour.
Pass Crème de Menthe to pour over fruit and ice.

WATERMELON SURPRISE—P

Cut watermelon in half, lengthwise.
Remove pulp. Fill 1/4 full with Raspberry Water Ice. Sprinkle with layer of semi-sweet chocolate bits. Alternate layers of water ice and chocolate bits. End with layer of water ice. Level off and insert chocolate bits to simulate seeds.
Serve in wedges with Angel Watermelon Cake.

Beverages

Orange Delight—D

4 cans frozen pineapple juice
12 cans water
1 pint orange sherbet
4 cans frozen lemon juice
4 lemon-juice cans of rum
4 lemon-juice cans of vodka
4 lemon-juice cans of Southern Comfort

Put in freezer until mushy. Blend.

Punch—D

Mix together in punch bowl:
4 cups pineapple juice
3 qts. lemonade
3 qts. orangeade
1 can crushed pineapple

When ready to serve add: **2 qts. raspberry soda**
Float scoops of: **1/2 gal. vanilla ice cream**

Passover

The holiday of Passover is one deeply rooted in our memories and hearts. It is a time for homecoming and nostalgic reminiscences of past Seders. We enjoy the sense of continuity which propels us back to the wondrous time of the Exodus and makes it a relevant happening for today. In keeping with the experience of uniting the past with the present, we have retained traditional recipes updated and have added dishes as modern as today, so that the nostalgia we create contains threads of the past, meaning for today, and memories for the future. We have been liberated from many of the limitations imposed upon us in the past by the restrictions of Passover, because of the variety of foods now on the market. So let's be creative, have fun, and add new dimension to the week of Passover.

APPLE CAKE—P

Serves ten.

In bowl, beat until stiff: **9 egg whites**

Set aside.

In bowl, beat until thick and light: **9 egg yolks**
1/2 cup sugar

Stir in: **9 T. matzo meal**
9 T. potato starch
juice and grated rind of lemon

Fold in: **egg whites**

Pour one-half batter into ungreased 9 × 13″ baking pan. Bake at 325°, 25 minutes.
Remove from oven and spread with apple mixture.

Apple Mixture

In bowl, combine: **6 apples, grated**
1/2 cup sugar
1 T. lemon juice
1 1/2 t. cinnamon

Spread remaining batter over apples. Bake 20–25 minutes longer, until brown.

APPLE CHARLOTTE—P

Serves six to eight.

In bowl, beat until thick and lemon-colored: **3 egg yolks**
2/3 cup sugar
pinch of salt

Stir in: **2 cups apples, grated**
1/3 cup matzo meal
2 t. lemon rind, grated
1 T. plum brandy

Fold in: **3 egg whites, stiffly beaten**

Turn into greased 8-inch spring form.

Sprinkle with: **4 T. pecans, ground**

Bake at 350°, 35 minutes or until brown and firm. Cool before removing sides of pan.

APPLE CRISP—P

Serves six.

In a bowl, combine: **6 apples, peeled, cored and sliced**
1/2 cup sugar
1/2 t. cinnamon
1/2 t. nutmeg
2 t. lemon juice

Pour into greased 1 1/2-quart casserole.

In bowl, blend to crumbly consistency: **1/2 cup sugar**
3/4 cup cake meal
1/8 t. salt
6 T. margarine

Add: **1/4 cup chopped nuts**

Sprinkle mixture over apples. Bake at 350° for 1 hour until crust is nicely browned. Serve hot.

APRICOT BARS—P

Sixteen pieces.

Soak: **1 cup dried apricots in**
1 cup boiling water

In bowl, beat together: **3 egg yolks**
3/4 cup sugar

Add:	**1 t. potato starch**
	1 cup nuts, chopped
	1 T. lemon juice
	pre-soaked apricots, drained and cut up
Fold in:	**3 egg whites, stiffly beaten**

Bake in greased 9-inch square pan at 350°, 40 minutes.

CASSEROLE OF MATZO AND CHICKEN—M

Serves four.

In bowl, beat until frothy:	**6 eggs**
Stir in:	**1/2 cup finely chopped onions**
	1/2 cup finely cut fresh dill or 2 T. dried dill
	1/4 cup finely chopped parsley
	2 t. salt
	freshly ground black pepper
Add:	**3 cups cooked chicken, in chunks**
In small sauce pan, heat:	**1/2 cup oil**

Pour 1 teaspoon of oil into an 8-inch square baking dish, tilting dish to spread it evenly.

To assemble, you will use:	**3 squares of matzo**
	2 cups chicken stock

Dip a square of matzo into chicken stock until it is well moistened. Place on bottom of baking dish. Spread one-half of chicken-egg mixture evenly over it. Dip second square of matzo in stock and place it over chicken. Spread remaining chicken-egg mixture on top and cover with third moistened matzo. Pour half remaining oil evenly over last matzo and bake at 400° in middle of oven for 15 minutes. Pour rest of oil on top and continue baking for 15 minutes longer, or until the top is nicely browned. Serve immediately.

CHIFFON PIES—P

Serve eight to ten.

Meringue Shell

In bowl, beat until stiff:	**3 egg whites**
Gradually beat in:	**1/2 cup sugar**
Beat in alternately:	**1/2 cup sugar**
	1 1/2 t. lemon juice or vinegar

Beat until very stiff and glossy. Spread in 9-inch pie plate. Bake at 275°, 60 minutes. Cool and fill.

Fillings

CHOCOLATE—**P**

In mixing bowl, beat until fluffy:	**1 cup margarine**
	3/4 cup sugar
Add:	**4 oz. bittersweet chocolate, melted and cooled**
Add one at a time, beating well after each addition:	**4 eggs**

Beat until thick and light-colored. Spoon into baked and cooled Meringue Shell. Refrigerate. Garnish with slivered almonds.

LEMON—**P**

In sauce pan, combine:	**3 egg yolks**
	6 T. sugar
	1/4 t. salt
Add and cook over low heat stirring until mixture boils:	**1/4 cup lemon juice, unstrained**

Remove from heat.

Beat in:	**4 T. lemon-flavored gelatin dissolved in**
	1/2 cup boiling water
	1 T. lemon rind, grated

Cool. When mixture is partially set, beat until smooth.

Fold into meringue of: **3 egg whites, beaten stiff**
6 T. sugar

Spoon into baked and cooled Meringue Shell. Chill until set, about 2 hours.

STRAWBERRY—**P**

In sauce pan, combine and cook over low heat, stirring until boiled: **3 egg yolks**
6 T. sugar
1/4 t. salt
2 t. lemon juice
1 cup crushed strawberries

Remove from heat.

Stir in mixture of: **4 T. strawberry-flavored gelatin**
2 T. hot strawberry juice

Cool.
When mixture is partially set, beat until smooth.

Fold into meringue of: **3 egg whites, beaten stiff**
6 T. sugar

Spoon into baked and cooled Meringue Shell. Chill until set, 2 hours. Garnish with large, choice fresh strawberries.

CHOCOLATE-ORANGE CAKE—P

Serves six.

In bowl, cream: **1/2 cup margarine**
2/3 cup sugar

Add, one at a time: **3 eggs**

The batter at this stage will look curdled, but don't be alarmed.

Stir in: **4 oz. semi-sweet chocolate, melted**
1 cup almonds, ground
rind of 1 large orange, grated
1 cup cake meal

Mix together and pour into 8-inch round cake pan, which has been greased, lined with waxed paper, and greased again. Bake at 375°, 25 minutes. Allow cake to cool on rack for 30 minutes, then run knife around edge, turn onto cake rack. Peel off waxed paper. Cool completely and glaze.
The center of the cake will seem quite soft. Do not be alarmed. This enhances its texture and flavor.

GLAZE

In sauce pan, combine: **4 oz. semi-sweet chocolate**
1/4 cup margarine
2 t. honey

Heat through until chocolate is melted. Remove from heat and beat until it thickens. Place cake (on the rack) over a piece of waxed paper and pour glaze over cake. Tip cake so that glaze runs evenly over top and down sides. Smooth sides if necessary. Garnish with toasted almonds. This cake freezes well.

CHOCOLATE-SPICE CAKE—P

Serves ten.

In bowl, beat until foamy: **5 egg whites**
Beat in: **1/4 cup sugar, 1 T. at a time**

Beat until whites form stiff peaks. Set aside.

In bowl, combine and beat until thick: **5 egg yolks**
2 whole eggs
1/4 cup sugar
Beat in: **1/2 t. cinnamon**
1 T. lemon rind, grated
3/4 cup grated almonds
1/3 cup grated chocolate

Mix 1/4 of egg whites into batter. Pour batter over rest of whites. Pour into 4 × 12″ loaf pan which has been greased well and dusted with

1/4 cup cake meal. Bake at 350° in middle of oven for 25–30 minutes or until golden brown and cake shrinks slightly away from sides of pan. Let cool for 2–3 minutes in pan and turn out on rack. When cool, glaze. For glaze, see above recipe for chocolate glaze. Garnish with 1 cup almonds.

FRUIT PUDDING—P

Serves ten.

Soak 5 squares of matzos in cold water.

In bowl, beat until stiff and set aside:	**5 egg whites**
In second bowl, beat:	**5 egg yolks**
	1 1/2 cups sugar
	3 apples, grated
	rind of 1 lemon
	juice of 1 orange
	1 t. cinnamon
	1/2 cup almonds, chopped
	1/2 cup raisins
	3 T. margarine, melted
Fold in:	**Beaten egg whites**
Fold in:	**matzos, drained**

Pour into greased 9 × 13″ baking dish. Set baking dish in pan of water and bake at 400°, 45 minutes. Serve with Wine Sauce.

Wine Sauce

In small bowl, beat and set aside:	**2 egg whites**
In second bowl, beat:	**2 egg yolks**
	1 whole egg
	1/4 cup sugar
Add mixture of:	**2 cups wine**
	1 T. potato flour
Fold in:	**Beaten whites**

Serve immediately or sauce will separate and thin.

HONEY CAKE—P

Serves ten to twelve.

In large mixing bowl, beat until thick and lemon-colored:	**3 eggs**
	1 cup sugar
In large measuring cup, mix together:	**1 cup strong coffee**
	1 cup honey
	2 t. allspice
	1 t. ginger
	1 t. baking soda
	1/4 cup oil

Stir gently into egg mixture.

Fold in:	**1 1/2 cup cake meal**
	1 cup potato starch
Add:	**1/2 cup raisins**
	1/2 cup chopped nuts

Pour into 9 × 13″ pan lined with waxed paper. Decorate with slivered almonds. Bake at 350°, 45 minutes or until cake tests done.

JELLY ROLL—P

Serves ten to twelve.

In bowl, beat 15 minutes:	**6 eggs**
	1 cup sugar
Fold in:	**1/2 cup cake meal**
	1/2 cup potato starch
	1 t. salt

Spread in 15 × 10 1/2″ waxed-paper-lined jelly roll pan. Bake at 350°, 20 minutes. Loosen edges and immediately turn upside down on towel sprinkled with sugar. Quickly and carefully remove waxed paper. Spread cake at once with soft jelly or jam and roll up.

LEMON MERINGUE CAKE—P

Place large sponge tube cake upside down on oven-proof dish. Slice entire top from cake about 1 inch down. Lift off top and lay to one side. Cut down into cake 1 inch from outer edge and 1 inch from middle hole. Remove center cake with spoon, leaving a wall of cake about 1 inch thick and a 1-inch base at bottom. Completely fill cavity with Lemon Filling. Replace top of cake and press gently. Cover top and sides with Meringue. Bake at 425°, 5–8 minutes, until brown. Watch carefully.

Lemon Filling

In sauce pan, combine: **1 1/2 cups sugar**
1 level T. potato starch
Gradually stir in: **1 1/2 cups water**

Cook over moderate heat, stirring constantly until mixture thickens and boils. Boil 1 minute.

Stir 1/2 hot mixture, slowly, into: **3 egg yolks, slightly beaten**

Beat into hot mixture in sauce pan. Boil 1 minute longer, stirring constantly. Remove from heat. Continue stirring until smooth.

Blend in: **3 T. margarine**
4 T. lemon juice
1 1/3 T. lemon rind, grated

Meringue-P

In small bowl, beat until frothy: **3 egg whites**
Gradually beat in: **6 T. sugar, one T. at a time**

Continue beating until stiff and glossy.

LINZERTORTE—P

Serves twelve.

In bowl, place: **1/2 cup cake meal**
1/2 cup potato starch

Cut in: **1 cup margarine**
Add: **1 1/2 cups unpeeled almonds, grated**
Add mixture of: **1/2 cup sugar**
1/2 t. cinnamon
2 egg yolks

Knead dough until smooth and well blended. Turn 2/3 of dough into ungreased 9-inch spring form. Press dough over bottom and half-way up sides.

Spread with: **1/3 cup raspberry jam**

Roll egg-sized balls of remaining dough between palms of hands to make long rolls about 1/3–1/2″ wide and 8″ long. Place rolls on baking sheet and bake until firm. Using spatula, lift rolls and arrange lattice-style over jam. Fasten to dough around rim of pan by pressing lightly.

Brush with: **Egg white, slightly beaten**

Bake at 325°, 1 hour and 15 minutes. Partly cool before removing rim of pan.

MACAROONS—P

Almond

Two dozen

In sauce pan, combine and cook, stirring constantly: **1 1/4 cups almonds, grated**
3/4 cup sugar
3 egg whites, unbeaten

Cook, but *do not boil,* until batter looks as thick as soft mashed potatoes, about 8–10 minutes.

Remove from heat and stir in: **1 T. lemon juice**

Drop by teaspoonfuls on two greased and lightly dusted cookie sheets. Let stand at room temperature about 1 hour to give macaroons a better shape. Bake at 300°, 20–25 minutes. Remove from cookie sheet immediately.

Chocolate

Two dozen

Follow directions for making Almond Macaroons.

Add to egg-white mixture in sauce pan:	**1/2 cup bittersweet chocolate bar broken into pieces**

Omit lemon juice.

Coconut

Two dozen

Follow directions for making Almond Macaroons.

Add to egg-white mixture in sauce pan:	**1/2 cup grated coconut**
Remove from heat and stir in:	**3 T. cake meal**
	1 t. lemon juice

MANDEL BREAD—P

Twenty-six 1-inch slices.

In bowl, beat until thick and lemon-colored:	**3 eggs**
	3/4 cup sugar
Stir in:	**1/2 cup oil**
Fold in:	**1 1/2 cups cake meal**
	1 T. potato starch

1/2 cup nuts, chopped
1/2 cup raisins
1/2 cup coconut

Spoon onto very lightly greased baking sheet and form into 2 long strips. Moisten hands and smooth strips into shape. Sprinkle top with cinnamon and sugar. Bake 350° for 30 minutes. When done cut into slices. If you prefer it drier, you may sprinkle individual slices with additional cinnamon and sugar and place back in 350° oven for 5 minutes.

MANDELTORTE—P

Serves twelve.

In bowl, beat until light:	**6 egg yolks**
Gradually add and continue to beat until creamy:	**1 cup sugar**
Beat in:	**3 T. lemon juice**
	1 t. lemon rind, grated
	1 t. cinnamon
Fold in:	**1 cup blanched almonds, grated**
	1/2 cup fine matzo crumbs
Fold in:	**6 egg whites, beaten stiff but not dry with**
	1/2 t. salt

Pour into two 8-inch layer pans, greased, bottoms lined with waxed paper and greased again. Bake at 350°, 40 minutes, until top is firm to touch. Invert pans on rack, cool and then remove cakes. Remove paper and fill layers with Lemon Filling. Frost with Honey Fluff Icing.

Lemon Filling-P

In sauce pan, combine and cook stirring until thick:	**2 1/2 T. lemon juice**
	6 T. orange juice
	1/3 cup water
	1/2 cup sugar
	2 T. potato starch
	1/8 t. salt

3 egg yolks
1/2 t. grated lemon rind

Cool.

Honey Fluff Icing-P

In bowl, beat until frothy: **3 egg whites**
1/4 t. salt

Gradually add and beat until smooth and glossy: **6 T. sugar**

Slowly add and beat until icing forms peaks: **6 T. honey**

Fold in: **1 t. grated lemon rind**

MARBLE CAKE—P

Serves ten to twelve.

In bowl, beat until stiff and set aside: **6 egg whites**
1 t. salt

In second bowl, beat: **6 egg yolks with**
scant cup sugar
juice of lemon

Fold in: **1/3 cup cake meal**
2 heaping T. potato starch
1 T. lemon rind, grated

Fold in: **Egg whites**

Spoon 2/3 of batter into ungreased 10-inch tube pan.

Fold into remaining batter mixture of: **1 1/2 oz. bittersweet chocolate melted with**
2 1/2 T. warm water

Pour here and there over sponge cake batter. Cut through batter with knife several times for marble effect. Bake at 325°, 40 minutes. Invert over soda bottle and let hang until cold.

297

·TZO FARFEL CUPS—P

Serves eight.

·owl, combine:	**1 cup matzo farfel**
	1 cup boiling water
	1 T. fat
	1 t. salt
Add:	**3 egg yolks, slightly beaten**
Fold in:	**1 apple, grated**
	1 t. cinnamon
	2 T. sugar
Fold in:	**3 egg whites, beaten stiff**

Spoon into well-greased muffin pans. Bake at 400°, 20–25 minutes.

MATZO MEAL PANCAKES—P

About two dozen.

In bowl, combine and beat:	**6 eggs**
	1 1/2 cups cold water
	2 t. salt
	2 T. sugar
Stir in:	**1 cup matzo meal**

Drop by tablespoon in hot fat in skillet. Fry quickly and brown on both sides. Serve immediately with cinnamon and sugar. For **D**, serve with sour cream.

PASSOVER PUFFS—P

Ten or eleven rolls.

In sauce pan, combine and bring to boil:	**2 T. sugar**
	1/2 cup peanut oil

	1 1/2 cups boiling water
Remove from heat and add:	**1 t. salt**
	1 1/2 cups matzo meal
	1/2 t. cinnamon (optional)

Blend until mixture forms ball.
Cool slightly.

Add one at a time, beating well after each addition:	**4 eggs**

Moisten hands. Shape batter into balls about 2–2 1/2 inches in diameter. Sprinkle with cinnamon and sugar. Bake at 375° 45 minutes, until brown.

SPONGE CAKE—P

Serves ten to twelve.

In bowl, beat until stiff and set aside:	**7 egg whites**
	1 t. salt
In second bowl, beat 20 minutes:	**7 egg yolks**
	2 whole eggs
	1 3/4 cups sugar
Add:	**juice and rind of 1 lemon**
Fold in:	**1/2 cup cake meal**
	1/2 cup potato starch
Fold in:	**Beaten egg whites**

Pour into 10-inch ungreased tube pan and bake at 325°, 1 hour. Invert over soda bottle and let hang until cold.

SPONGE CAKE WITH FRUIT—P

Serves eight to ten.

In bowl, beat until foamy:	**3 egg whites**
	pinch of salt
Add and beat to stiff peaks:	**1/2 cup sugar, 1 T. at a time**
In second bowl, beat lightly:	**3 egg yolks**
	1/2 t. grated lemon peel
	2 t. lemon juice
	1 t. orange juice

Mix 1/4 beaten whites into egg yolks. Then pour yolk mixture over whites.

Sprinkle and fold in:	**1/4 cup cake meal**
	1/4 cup potato starch

Pour batter into greased 9-inch layer cake pan.

Spread over top:	**1 cup canned fruit, drained**

Bake at 350°, 35–40 minutes until golden brown. Cool in pan.

STUFFING—P

In bowl, combine and blend:	**4 matzos broken into bits**
	1/2 cup cold water
	1 medium onion, grated
	2 T. fat
	1/2 t. salt
	pepper
	1/2 t. sugar
	2 eggs
	1 T. parsley

Use to fill cavity of turkey or capon.

THUMBPRINT COOKIES—P

About two dozen.

In bowl, combine:
1/2 cup oil
1/2 cup sugar
2 eggs
3/4 cup cake meal
1 cup nuts, chopped
1 t. lemon juice

Drop by teaspoonful on greased cookie sheet. Make indentation with thumb in center of cookie batter. Bake at 450°, 5–8 minutes. Fill indentation with bright-colored jam.

TZIMMES—M

Serves twelve.

In skillet, heat and brown:
1 lb. flanken, or top of rib
2 onions, diced

In sauce pan, combine:
2 packages (large) frozen carrots
1 package frozen squash
2–3 sweet potatoes, peeled and cut in chunks
2 T. sugar
2 T. honey
salt and pepper to taste
water to cover

Partially cook. Transfer meat and vegetables to roasting pan.

To the liquid in sauce pan, add:
1 T. potato starch
1 T. sugar
salt and pepper

Pour liquid over meat and vegetables. Bake at 325° 2 hours.
Optional but good added to the tzimmes before baking:
Stuffed poultry-neck skin
Clean and scrape the skin of the poultry neck. Do not cut away the fat. Sew or tie one end to keep in the stuffing.

Stuffing

In bowl, combine:

1 medium-sized potato, grated
1/2 cup matzo meal
1 small onion, grated
salt and pepper to taste
2 t. sugar
2 T. chicken fat, cut in pieces

Stuff neck loosely, one-half full to allow for expansion. Sew or tie end. Shake to distribute stuffing evenly.

For dumplings, cook matzo knaidel in water, drain, and add to tzimmes.

Index

Acorn Squash, 139
Almond (s)
  Chocolate Tarts, 240
  Macaroons, 294–95
  Mandel Bread, 217, 295
  Mandeltorte, 296
  Rolla Cake, 248–49
Angel-Watermelon Cake, 187–88
Antipasto, 150–51
Appetizers:
  Blintzes, 37–38
  Cabbage, rolled, 38–39
  Caviar
    Mold, 39–40
    Pie, 40
    Platter, 40–41
  Cheese
    Fondue, 41
    Rounds, 41
  Cherry Tomatoes
    Marinated, 41–42
    Stuffed, 42
  Chicken Crêpes, 43
  Chili Meat Pies, 43–44
  Cream Cheese Roll-ups, 45
  Cream Puffs, 45
  Cucumber, Filled, 47
  Eggs
    Deviled, 45–46
    Rancho, 46
  Fish
    Crêpes, 47–48
    Gefulte, 49
    Gormanese, 49–50
    Remoulade, 50
  Giblets with Meat Balls, 50
  Greek Hors d'Oeuvres, 51–52
  Guacamole, 52
  Herring
    à l'Étoile, 53
    Chopped, 53
  Hot Dogs, Sweet and Sour, 53
  Knishes, 54
  Knockwurst, Pickled, 54–55
  Kreplach, 55
  Liver, Chopped, 55–56
  Meat Ball Variations, 56–58
  Melon Variations, 58
  Mock Pizza, 61–62
  Mock Seafood Cocktail, 66
  Mushroom(s)
    Fried, 58
    Quiche, 63
    Roll-ups, 59
    Stuffed, 59–60
  Onion Dip, 60
  Pineapple-Cheese Lollypops, 60
  Pinwheel Sandwiches, 60–61
  Pizza
    Mock, 61–62
    Roll-ups, 62

Potato Pancakes, 62
Quiche Lorraine, 63
Salami, Baked, 37
Salmon Croquettes, 64–65
Sardine Spread, 65
Smoked Salmon Roll-ups, 65
Spinach Quiche, 64
Sushi, 66
Tomatoes Stuffed with Liver, 66–67
Tuna
Cheese Spread, 67
Pâté, 67–68
Won Ton, Fried, 68
Apple (s)
Blintzes, 253
Cake, 188, 284
Charlotte, 284–85
Crisp, 249–50, 285
Muffins, 174–75
Pie, 234
French, 241
Squares, 250
Strudel, 206–07
Tuna Salad with, 124
Waldorf Salad, 162
Applesauce, 189–90
Apricot
Bars, 285–86
Glaze, 228
Mold, 155
Nut Bread, 171
Sauce, 209
Soufflé, 267–68
Strips, 207–08
Artichoke
Tomato Salad, 162
Asparagus Vinaigrette, 139–40

Baba au Rhum, 251
Baked Alaska, 274–75
Baklava, 252–53
Banana Soufflé, 268
Barbecued Short Ribs, 92–93
Barbecue Sauce, 57, 178
Barley Pilaf, 126
Bavarian Pie à la Joftes, 236
Bean Sprouts, 140
Béarnaise Sauce, 179
Beef
Bourguignonne, 77
Brisket
Cape Cod, 88
Carbonnade of, 88–89
Glazed Corned, 89
Sweet and Sour, 90
Chinese, 78
Fondue, 78–79
and Fried Rice Casserole, 93
Ground
Beef Pastries, 81–82
Chili Meat Pies, 43–44
Giblets with Meat Balls, 50
Kreplach, 55
Meat Ball Variations, 56–57
Shepherd's Pie, 90–91
Spaghetti and Meat Balls, 91–92
Stuffing for Crown Lamb Roast, 97
Hot Dogs
and Beans Casserole, 93–94
Split Pea Soup with, 75–76
Sweet and Sour, 53
Italian, 80
Ka-Bobs, 80–81
London Broil, 86
in Marinated Mushrooms, 81
Pastries, 81–82
in Red Wine, 82
Roast, 85–86
Sauerbraten, 89–90
Savory, with Vegetables, 82–83
Sherried, 83
Short Ribs, Barbecued, 92–93
Spanish, 84–85
Steak
Beef in Marinated Mushrooms, 81–82
Planked, 86–87
Teriyaki, 85
Tongue, Sweet and Sour, 94
Top of Rib, Stuffed, 87
Beets
Harvard, 140
Hawaiian, 140
Beignets Soufflés, 208–09
Belmont Sweet Rolls, 176
Beverages:
Orange Delight, 282

Punch, 282
Bird's Nest Cookies, 209–10
Bisque Tortoni, 275–76
Blackberry Chiffon Pie, 240
Blintzes, 37–38
Apple, 253
Blueberry, 253
Blueberry
Blintzes, 253
Coffee Cake, 194–95
Muffins, 175
Pie, 236–37
Squares, 250
Bourbon Cake, 254
Brandied Fruit, 151
Breads:
Apricot-Nut, 171
Belmont Sweet Rolls, 176–77
Cinnamon Twists, 177
Date-Nut, 172
Garlic, 127
Orange Honey, 172–73
Sweet-Dough Yeast, 173–74
Breaded Veal Steak, 94
Broccoli
Medley, 142
Ring, 142–43
Brownies
Blonde, 210
Chocolate, 211–12
Brunch menus:
dairy, 3–5
meat, 4, 5
Buffet menus:
dairy, 30
meat, 29–30
Bundt Cake, 190
Burgundy Mold, 156

Cabbage
Rolled, 38–39
Soup, Sweet and Sour, 69

Caesar Salad, 151
Cakes:
Almond Rolla, 248–49
Angel-Watermelon, 187–88
Apple, 188, 284
Applesauce, 189–90
Blueberry Coffee, 194–95
Bourbon, 254
Bundt, 190
Caramel, 191
Cherry-Nut Chiffon, 191–92
Chiffon
Cherry-Nut, 191–92
Chocolate Chip, 192–93
Orange, 193
Chocolate
Devil's Food, 193–94
Orange, 289
Spice, 289–90
Syrup, 194
Velvet, 273
Chocolate Chip Chiffon, 192–93
Coffee
Blueberry, 194–95
French Orange, 195
Sour Cream, 196
Devil's Food, 193–94
Dobosch Torte, 196–98
French Orange Coffee, 195
Fruit, 198
Torte, 198–99
Genoise, 199–200
Hazelnut, 200–01
Honey, 201, 291
Italian Loaf, 262–63
Marble, 297
Orange, 201–02
Chiffon, 193
French Coffee, 195
Pineapple Upside-Down, 202
Pound, 203
Pumpkin, 204
Sacher Torte, 204–05
Sour Cream Coffee, 196
Sponge, 205, 299
with Fruit, 300
Strawberry, 268
Velvet Chocolate, 273
Cape Cod Brisket, 88
Caramel
Cake, 191
Icing, 228
Carbonnade of Brisket, 88–89

Carrot (s)
  Rings, 143–44
  Soufflé, 143
Casseroles:
  Beef Bourguignonne, 77
  Chicken and Matzo, 286
  Fried Rice and Beef, 93
  Hot Dogs and Beans, 93–94
  Italian Beef, 80
  Spanish Beef, 84–85
  Top of Rib, Stuffed, 87
  Veal, 95
Cauliflower
  Mock Seafood Cocktail, 66
  in Mushroom Sauce, 144
Caviar
  Mold, 39–40
  Pie, 40
  Platter, 40–41
  Salad Dressing, 179
Champagne Sauce, 117
Chasseur Sauce, 114
Cheese
  Balls, 160
  Blintzes, 37–38
  Cream Cheese Roll-ups, 45
  Fondue, 41
  Lasagna Lenora, 124–25
  Pineapple Lollypops, 60
  Rounds, 41
  Squares, 210–11
  Tarts, 237
  Torte, 254–55
  Tuna Spread, 67
Cherry (ies)
  Jubilee, 255
  Nut Chiffon Cake, 191–92
  Orange Sauce, 180
  Pie, 238
  Soup, Sour, 75
Cherry Tomatoes
  Marinated, 41–42
  Stuffed, 42
Chicken
  Breasts in Rosé Wine, 98
  Chasseur, 98–99
  and Cherries, 99
  Chinese, 99–100
  Chinese Fried, 100–1
  Coq au Vin, 110–11
  Crêpes, 43
  in Crumbs, 101
  Curry, 101–2
  Fried, 102
  with Fruit Medley, 102–3
  in Grapes and Oranges, 103–4
  Hawaiian, 104
  with Honey and Mustard, 105
  Kiev, 105
  à la King, 106
  and Kumquats, 106–7
  Lime-Broiled, 107
  and Matzo Casserole, 286
  in Pineapple Boats, 107–8
  in Rice, 108–9
  Salad, 109
  Sherried, on Green Noodles, 109–10
  Soup with Matzo Balls, 70
  in Sweet and Sour Sauce, 110
Chiffon:
  Cakes:
    Cherry-Nut, 191–92
    Chocolate Chip, 192–93
    Orange, 193
  Pies:
    Blackberry, 240
    Chocolate, 238–39, 287
    Lemon, 239, 287
    Mocha, 239
    Raspberry, 240
    Strawberry, 288
Chili
  Meat Pies, 43–44
  Sauce, 56
Chinese
  Beef, 78
  Chicken, 99–100
  Fried Chicken, 100–1
  Sauce, 56
Chocolate
  Balls, 211
  Brownies, 211–12
  Cakes
    Devil's Food, 193–94
    Orange, 289
    Spice, 289–90
    Syrup, 194
    Velvet, 273

- Crumb Crust, 275
- Cups, 255–56
- Delight Bars, 212
- Filling, 259
- Frosting, 229
- Icing, 229
- Macaroons, 295
- Mousse, 256–57
- Pie, 240
  - Chiffon, 238–39
- Roll, 257
- Sauce, 266–67
- Tarts
  - Almond, 240
  - Quick, 246
- Triple Squares, 226–27
- Upside-Down Dessert, 276

Chocolate Chip Chiffon Cake, 192–93
Cinnamon Twists, 177
Citrus Soup, Frappé, 71
Cocktail party menus:
- dairy, 11–12
- meat, 11

Coconut Macaroons, 295
Coffee Cakes:
- Blueberry, 194–95
- French Orange, 195
- Sour Cream, 196

Coffee-Marshmallow Dessert, 258
Cognac Filling, 229–30
Cole Slaw, 152
Confectioner's Sugar Icing, 230
Cookies and Small Pastries:
- Apple
  - Squares, 250
  - Strudel, 206–07
- Apricot Strips, 207–08
- Beignets Soufflés, 208–09
- Bird's Nest Cookies, 209–10
- Blonde Brownies, 210
- Blueberry Squares, 250
- Cheese Squares, 210–11
- Chocolate
  - Balls, 211
  - Brownies, 211–12
  - Delight Bars, 212
- Date
  - Balls, 213
  - Bars, 213
- Filled Cookies, 214
- Frosted Tinted Cookies, 214–15
- Graham Cracker Squares, 215
- Jelly Rolls, 215, 291
- Lace Cookies, 216
- Lemon Drops, 216
- Mandel Bread, 217
- Marble
  - Bars, 217–18
  - Squares, 218
- Mock Strudel, 218–19
- Molasses Cookies, 219
- Neapolitan Cookies, 219–20
- Pineapple Layer Bars, 220–21
- Raisin Ginger Snaps, 221–22
- Raspberry Bars, 222
- Sarah's Sour Cream Roll-ups, 222–23
- Scotch Toffee, 223
- Strudel, 223–24
- Taiglach, 224–25
- Thumbprint Cookies, 225–26, 301
- Triple Chocolate Squares, 226–27

Coq au Vin, 110–11
Cranberry
- Celery Mold, 156
- Orange Relish, 152
- Water Ice, 279–80

Cream Cheese Roll-ups, 45
Cream Puffs, 45
Creamy Frosting, 230
Crêpes
- Chicken, 43
- with Chocolate Filling, 259
- Fish, 47–48, 115–16
- Suzette, 258–59

Crown Lamb Roast, 97
Cucumber
- Filled, 47
- Salad, 153

Cumberland Sauce, 180

Date
- Balls, 213
- Bars, 213
- Nut Bread, 172

Dessert Pears, 260
Deviled Eggs, 45–46
Devil's Food Cake, 193–94

Dinner menus:
dairy, 21–23, 26
meat, 13–21, 23, 24–26, 27–28
Dobosch Torte, 196–98
Duck à l'Orange, 112

Eggplant, Fried, 144
Eggs
Deviled, 45–46
Foo Yong, 162
Omelets, 169–70
Rancho, 46
Scrambled, 166–67
Zabaglione, 186.
See also Soufflés

Filled Cookies, 214
Fillings:
Chocolate, 259
Cognac, 229–30
Lemon, 293, 296–97. *See also* Frostings
Fish
Chasseur, 114
Chowder, 71, 73
Crêpes, 47–48, 115–16
Fried, English Style, 116
Gefulte, 49
Gormanese, 49–50
Mousse, 117
Remoulade, 50
Rolled Stuffed, 119
Salad, 117–18
Stock, 118. *See also* individual varieties
French Apple Pie, 241
French Orange Coffee Cake, 195
Frosted Grapes, 281
Frosted Tinted Cookies, 214–15
Frostings:
Apricot Glaze, 228
Caramel Icing, 228
Chocolate, 229
Icing, 229
Confectioner's Sugar Icing, 230
Creamy, 230
Honey Fluff Icing, 297
Mocha, 231
Orange, 231–32
Quick, 232
Snowy White, 232
Frozen Desserts:
Baked Alaska, 274–75
Bisque Tortoni, 275–76
Chocolate Upside-Down Dessert, 276
Cranberry Water Ice, 279–80
Fruit Water Ice, 280
Ice Cream Soufflé, 277
Lemon Ice with Frosted Grapes, 280–81
Meringue Shells with Zabaglione Sauce, 277–78
Orange-Raspberry Baskets, 278
Tangerine Surprise, 279
Watermelon Surprise, 281
Fruit
Brandied, 151
Cake, 198
Compote, Hot, 153
Plates, 261
Pudding, 290
Sauce for Meat, 103
Tarts, 241
Torte, 198–99, 261
Water Ice, 280

Garlic
Bread, 127
Sauce, 79
Gazpacho, 73
Gefulte Fish, 49
Genoise, 199–200
German Pancakes, 130
Giblets with Meat Balls, 50
Ginger Ale Salad Mold, 157
Glazed Corned Brisket, 89
Glazed Oranges, 263–64
Graham Cracker Squares, 215
Grapes, Frosted, 281
Greek Hors D'Oeuvres, 51–52
Green Bean Salad, 154
Guacamole, 52

Haddock
Baked, 119
Flaked, Remoulade, 120
Hawaiian Chicken, 104
Hazelnut Cake, 200–01

Herring
à l'Étoile, 53
Chopped, 53
Kippered, 120
Honey
Baklava, 252–53
Cake, 201
Fluff Icing, 297
Orange Bread, 172–73
Orange Muffins, 175–76
Taiglach, 224–25
Horseradish
Sauce, 79
Squares, Frozen, 181
Hot Dogs
and Beans Casserole, 93–94
Split Pea Soup with, 75–76
Sweet and Sour, 53

Ice Cream Soufflé, 277
Ices
Cranberry Water, 279–80
Fruit Water, 280
Lemon, 280–81
Icings. *See* Frostings
Italian Beef, 80
Italian Loaf Cake, 262–63

Jelly Rolls, 215, 291

Kahlúa Pie, 242
Kippered Herring, 120
Knishes, 54
Knockwurst, Pickled, 54
Kreplach, 55

Lace Cookies, 216
Lamb
Crown Roast, 97
Ka-Bobs, 97
Lasagna Lenora, 124–25
Late supper menus:
dairy, 31–32
meat, 32
pareve, 32
Lemon
Drops, 216
Fillings, 293, 296–97
Ice with Frosted Grapes, 280–81
Mayonnaise, 181
Meringue Cake, 293
Pie
Chiffon, 239
Meringue, 243
Sauce, 181–82
Lime
Mold, 157–58
Pie
Meringue, 244
Pineapple, 244
Linzertorte, 293–94
Liver
Chopped, 55–56
Tomatoes Stuffed with, 66–67
London Broil, 86–87
Lox. *See* Salmon, Smoked
Luncheon menus
dairy, 6–8
meat, 8–9

Macaroons
Almond, 294–95
Chocolate, 295
Coconut, 295
Mandel Bread, 217, 295
Mandeltorte, 296
Marble
Bars, 217–18
Cake, 295
Squares, 218
Marinades, 54, 85, 86, 92, 94, 96, 97. *See also* Sauces
Marinated Pineapple, 264
Marinated Veal Chops, 96
Marmalade Barbecue Sauce, 57
Marshmallow
Coffee Dessert, 258
Matzo
Balls, 70
and Chicken Casserole, 286
Farfel Cups, 298
Meal Pancakes, 298
Meat Balls
Chili, 56
Chinese, 56–57
Horseradish, 57
Spaghetti and, 91–92
Melon Variations, 58

Menus:
brunch, 3–5
buffet, 29–30
cocktail party, 11–12
dinner, 13–28
late supper, 31–32
luncheon, 6–9
Saturday afternoon kiddush, 33–34
tea, 10
Meringue Shells with Zabaglione Sauce, 277
Minestrone, 74
Mixed Green Salad, 155
Mocha
Chiffon Pie, 239
Frosting, 231
Mock Pizza, 61–62
Mock Seafood Cocktail, 66
Mock Strudel, 218–19
Molasses Cookies, 219
Molds:
Apricot, 155
Broccoli Ring, 142–43
Burgundy, 156
Carrot Rings, 143–44
Caviar, 39–40
Cranberry-Celery, 156
Ginger Ale Salad, 157
Lime, 157–58
Orange, 158
Red, White and Blue, 158–59
Strawberry-Cheese, 159–60
Strawberry-Rhubarb, 160
Muffins:
Apple, 174–75
Blueberry, 175
Orange Honey, 175–76
Mushroom (s)
Beef in Marinated, 81
Cauliflower in Mushroom Sauce, 144
Fried, 58
Quiche, 63
Roll-ups, 59
Sauce, 182
Soufflé, 167–68
Stuffed, 59

Neapolitan Cookies, 219–20
Noodle (s)
Poppy Seed, 127
Pudding, 127–29

Onion (s)
Curried, 183
Dip, 60
Rings, Sautéed, 183
Orange (s)
Cake, 201–02
Chiffon, 193
French Coffee, 195
Cranberry Relish, 152
Delight, 282
Filling, 231
Frosting, 231–32
Glazed, 263–64
Honey Bread, 172–73
Honey Muffins, 175–76
Minted Peas, 144–45
Mold, 158
Raspberry Baskets, 278

Pancakes:
German, 130
Matzo Meal, 298
Potato, 62
Paris Chou, 264–66
Passover Puffs, 298-99
Passover Recipes, 283-302
Pears, Dessert, 260
Peas
Orange-Minted, 144–45
Spiced, 145
Pecan
Cups, 245
Pie, 245–46
Pie Crust, 233–34
Pies:
Apple, 234
French Apple, 241
Bavarian à la Joftes, 236
Blackberry Chiffon, 240
Blueberry, 236–37
Cherry, 238
Chiffon:
Blackberry, 240

Chocolate, 238–39
Lemon, 239
Mocha, 239
Raspberry, 240
Chocolate, 240
Chiffon, 238–39
French Apple, 241
Kahlúa, 242
Lemon
Chiffon, 239
Meringue, 243
Lime
Meringue, 244
Pineapple, 244
Mocha Chiffon, 239
Pecan, 245–46
Raspberry Chiffon, 240
Strawberry Flan, 246–47
Pineapple
Cheese Lollypops, 60
Chicken in Pineapple Boats, 107–8
Layer Bars, 220–21
Lime Pie, 244
Marinated, 264
Upside-Down Cake, 202
Pinwheel Sandwiches, 60–61
Piquant Sauce, 184
Pizza
Mock, 61–62
Roll-ups, 62
Planked Steak, 86–87
Popovers, 130
Potato (es)
Baked Stuffed, 131
French-Fried, 131–32
Oven-Fried, 132
Pancakes, 62
Pudding, 132–33
Salad, 161
Viennese, 134–35
Pound Cake, 203
Praline Cream, 265
Profiterole, 266–67
Puddings:
Fruit, 290
Noodle, 127–29
Potato, 132–33
Surprise, 271–72
Yorkshire, 138
Pumpkin Cake, 204
Punch, 282

Quiches:
Lorraine, 63
Mushroom, 63
Salmon, 121
Spinach, 64
Quick Frosting, 232
Quick Tarts, 246

Raisin Ginger Snaps, 221–22
Raspberry
Bars, 222
Chiffon Pie, 240
Orange Baskets, 278
Sauce, 209
Trifle, 272
Ratatouille, 145–46
Red, White and Blue Mold, 158–59
Remoulade Sauce, 184
Rice
Fried, 135
Pilaf, 136
Risotto d'Angelo, 135
Spanish, 136
Strauss, 137
Risotto d'Angelo, 135
Roast Beef, 85–86
Rock Cornish Hen, 113
Rosé Sauce, 98

Sacher Torte, 204–05
Salads:
Caesar, 151
Chicken, 109
Cole Slaw, 152
Cucumber, 153
Fish, 117–18
Green Bean, 154
Mixed Green, 155
Potato, 161
Tomato-Artichoke, 162
Tuna with Apples, 124
Variations, 161–62
Waldorf, 162
Waterford, 163

Salami, Baked, 37
Salmon
  Cold, 120
  Croquettes, 64–65
  Quiche, 121
  Sauce, 184–85
  Toast Cups, 121–22
Salmon, smoked
  Roll-ups, 65
  and Salmon Soufflé, 167
Sarah's Sour Cream Roll-ups, 222–23
Sardine Spread, 15
Saturday afternoon kiddush menus (meat), 33–34
Sauces and Dressings:
  Apricot, 209
  Barbecue, 57, 178
  Béarnaise, 178
  Caviar, Red, 179
  Champagne, 117
  Chasseur, 114
  Cherry-Orange, 180
  Chili, 56
  Chinese, 56
  Chocolate, 266–67
  Cumberland, 180
  Fruit, for Meat, 103
  Garlic, 79
  Horseradish, 79
  Horseradish Squares, Frozen, 181
  Lemon Mayonnaise, 181
  Lemon Sauce, 181–82
  Marmalade Barbecue, 57
  Mushroom, 182
  Onion, Curried, 183
  Piquant, 184
  Raspberry, 209
  Remoulade, 184
  Rosé, 98
  Salmon, 184–85
  Strawberry, 209
  Tomato, 79
  Velvet, 185
  Vinaigrette, 186
  Wine, 290
  Zabaglione, 186
Sauerbraten, 89–90
Savory Beef with Vegetables, 82–83
Scotch Toffee, 223
Shepherd's Pie, 90–91
Sherried Beef, 83
Sherried Chicken on Green Noodles, 109–10
Sherried Spinach, 146
Small Pastries. *See* Cookies and Small Pastries
Snowy White Frosting, 232
Soufflés:
  Apricot, 267–68
  Banana, 268
  Carrot, 143
  Ice Cream, 277
  Mushroom, 167–68
  Lox-Salmon, 167
Sole, Rolled Filet, 122
Soups:
  Cabbage, Sweet and Sour, 69
  Chicken, with Matzo Balls, 70
  Citrus, Frappé, 71
  Fish Chowder, 71, 73
  Gazpacho, 73
  Minestrone, 74
  Sour Cherry, 75
  Split Pea, with Sliced Hot Dogs, 75–76
  Tomato, Creamed with Peanuts, 76
Sour Cherry Soup, 75
Sour Cream
  Coffee Cake, 196
  Roll-ups, Sarah's, 222–23
Spaghetti and Meat Balls, 91–92
Spanish Beef, 84
Spanish Rice, 137
Spinach
  Quiche, 64
  Sherried, 146
Split Pea Soup with Sliced Hot Dogs, 75–76
Sponge Cake, 206, 299
  with Fruit, 300
Starches:
  Barley Pilaf, 126
  Bread, Garlic, 127
  Noodle(s)
    Poppy Seed, 127
    Pudding, 127–29
  Pancakes, German, 130
  Popovers, 130

Potato(es)
Baked Stuffed, 131
French-Fried, 131–32
Oven-Fried, 132
Pudding, 132–33
Viennese, 134–35
Rice
Fried, 135
Pilaf, 136
Risotto d'Angelo, 135
Spanish, 136
Strauss, 137
Sweet Potatoes
Candied, 133
in Orange Baskets, 133–34
Wild Rice Ring, 137
Yorkshire Pudding, 138
Strawberry (ies)
Cake, 268
Cheese Mold, 159–60
Flan, 246–47
Rhubarb Mold, 160
Romanoff, 271
Sauce, 209
Tarts, 246
String Beans
Amandine, 146
with Anchovies, 147
Strudel, 223–24
Apple, 206–07
Mock, 218–19
Stuffings, 300, 302
Summer Vegetable Platter, 147–48
Surprise Pudding, 271–72
Sushi, 66
Sweet and Sour Brisket, 90
Sweet and Sour Tongue, 94
Sweet Dough Yeast Breads, 173–74
Sweet Potatoes
Candied, 133
in Orange Baskets, 133–34
Swordfish Ka-Bobs, 123

Taiglach, 224–25
Tarts:
Cheese, 237
Chocolate
Almond, 240
Quick, 246
Fruit, 241
Pecan Cups, 245
Quick, 246
Strawberry, 246
Tangerine Surprise, 279
Tea menus, 10
Teriyaki, 85
Thumbprint Cookies, 225–26, 301
Toast Cups, 122
Tomato (es)
Artichoke Salad, 162
Broiled, 148
Sauce, 79
Soup, Creamed with Peanuts, 76
Stuffed with Liver, 66–67
Tongue, Sweet and Sour, 94
Top of Rib, Stuffed, 87
Trifle, 272
Triple Chocolate Squares, 226–27
Tuna
Cheese Spread, 67
Pâté, 67–68
Salad with Apples, 124
Turkey, Stuffed, 113–14
Tzimmes, 301–02

Veal
Casserole, 95
Chops, Marinated, 96
Sautéed with White Wine, 96
Steak, Breaded, 94
Vegetable Platter, Summer, 147–48
Velvet Chocolate Cake, 273
Velvet Sauce, 185
Vinaigrette Sauce, 186

Waldorf Salad, 162
Waterford Salad, 163
Watermelon Surprise, 281
Wild Rice Ring, 137
Wine Sauce, 290
Won Ton, Fried, 68

Yorkshire Pudding, 138

Zabaglione Sauce, 186
Zucchini, 148–49